LIGHT THEIR FIRE

Using Internal Marketing to

Ignite Employee Performance

and WOW Your Customers

Susan M. Drake
Michelle J. Gulman
Sara M. Roberts

Dearborn™
Trade Publishing
A **Kaplan Professional** Company

This publication is designed to provide accurate and authoritative information in regard to the subject matter covered. It is sold with the understanding that the publisher is not engaged in rendering legal, accounting, or other professional service. If legal advice or other expert assistance is required, the services of a competent professional person should be sought.

President, Dearborn Publishing: Roy Lipner
Vice President and Publisher: Cynthia A. Zigmund
Acquisitions Editor: Michael Cunningham
Senior Managing Editor: Jack Kiburz
Interior Design: Lucy Jenkins
Cover Design: Design Literate
Typesetting: Elizabeth Pitts

© 2005 by Susan M. Drake

Published by Dearborn Trade Publishing
A Kaplan Professional Company

All rights reserved. The text of this publication, or any part thereof, may not be reproduced in any manner whatsoever without written permission from the publisher.

Printed in the United States of America

05 06 07 08 10 9 8 7 6 5 4 3 2 1

ISBN: 978-1-60714-978-1

Kaplan Publishing books are available at special quantity discounts to use for sales promotions, employee premiums, or educational purposes. For more information or to purchase books, please call the Simon & Schuster special sales department at 866-506-1949.

DEDICATIONS

Susan's Dedication

To Scott, to my "Angels," who remind me it's important to be an idealist, and, as always, to Susan Gross, who knows when to bring chocolate.

Michelle's Dedication

To the family that lights my life, Tom, Judy, and Russell, and to my darling divas, Susan and Sara, for your generosity, love, and the pajama parties.

Sara's Dedication

To Susan Drake, I can't imagine my life today without you in it. I'm the luckiest person in the world to have been touched by your amazing gifts of intellect and friendship. You are an amazing mentor, a beautiful person, and a smart, smart cookie. You are internal marketing.

To Michelle Gulman, I am so honored to be a part of the "dynamic duo." Thanks for your friendship.

To my wonderful grandmother, Mary Ann, thank you for believing in me and helping me to reach the highest of heights. Without you, I just wouldn't be the person I am today.

To my late grandfather, Robert, you never failed to show me your undying love and support. If only everyone could be as amazing as you.

And to my mother, Barb, you deserve all the best things in the world. Your caring soul has shaped me far more than you even know.

Contents

PREFACE xi
ACKNOWLEDGMENTS xv
ABOUT THE AUTHORS xvii

1. **THE HOT TOPIC OF INTERNAL MARKETING** 1
   What Is Internal Marketing? 3
      Promises, Promises 4
   True Love or Lip Service? 5
      Two Ways to Sell the Promise 6
      From Train Wreck to Triple Crown 6
      The Flip Side 10
   It Starts with Culture 11
      It's Still about Walking the Talk 12
      A Tale of Two Organizations 12
   The "E" Factor 14
   How Do You Create an "E" Environment? 16
      How to Engage 17
      How to Enable 19
      How to Empower 22
      How to Ensure 23
   How Do Employees Contribute to Accomplishing Business Goals? 25
   Do You Need Internal Marketing? 27
      What If Yours Is Not a Big Corporation? 27

2. **WHY LIGHT THEIR FIRE?** *The Benefits of Internal Marketing* 31
   Fire That Gives Life: Why Internal Marketing Is Crucial to Business Performance 33
   Internal Marketing Creates "E" Employees 34
   Can't Buy Me Love: It Takes More than Pay to Make People Stay 36
   Burnout: The Expensive Cost of Not Marketing to Employees 37
   Fired Up: The Enormous Value of High Performance 39
      "E" Employees Earn Their Keep 39
      "E" Employees Go Beyond the Call of Duty 40

Fewer People Can Do More   40
"E" Employees Raise the Performance of an Entire Group   41
A Miserable Success   42
When Those Who Are Led Lead   43

"E" Employees Wow Customers   44
"E" Employees Wow Your Customers   44
And When They're Not, They're Horrid   46

The Sum of the Parts Is Extraordinary   48

3. BRAND POWER *Creating an Internal Brand*   51

Being a Beautiful Brand   52

Playing with Matches: How Internal Branding Lights Their Fire   54
Create Awareness and Consistency   54
Sustain a Positive Culture   56
Drive Change   57
Attract and Retain the Best Talent   59

Creating an Internal Brand   59
Be Persistent and Consistent   61
What Should Your Brand Look Like?   62
How to Create a Powerful Internal Marketing Campaign for
   Your Initiative   63

Brand Fanatics   64

Quiz: Are You "Selling" Your Company to Employees?   66

4. DOING YOUR HOMEWORK   71

Digging for Treasure   72

Step 1: Set a Course from A to B   72
Analyze the Situation   72
Strengths   73
Weaknesses   74
Opportunities   75
Threats   76

Goal for It! Setting Your Goals and Objectives   79
Creating Goals   80
Creating Objectives   80

Step 2: Know Your Audiences   82
Maslow's Hierarchy of Needs   83
Vary Your Audience by Message and Vary Your Message by Audience   84
Positioning Is Not Little White Lies   85

Target Practice   87
Direct Effect   87
The Poor Second or Third Shift   88

Off-site Workers 88
People Who Work for You but Don't Work for You 89
Contract Workers 91
Step 3: Assess the Climate 91
The Fun Begins 93

5. WHAT TO SAY TO WHOM AND HOW 95

Step 4: Define Your Key Messages 96
Perspective: Seeing Things from Your Audience's Point of View 96
The Subject Is "You" 98
Dealing with Good News and Bad News 99
A Few Suggestions for Communicating Bad News 101
Step 5: Match Vehicles to the Message 102
Appeal to the Right "Learning Channel" 103
Which Vehicles for Which Information? 105
Mission, Vision, and Values 105
Motivational Information 107
Strategic Information 108
Recognition of Team Members' Accomplishments 108
Company News 109
Financial Information 111
Detailed Factual Information 111
Detailed Training 111
Management Directives 112
How to Make the Most of Your Communication Vehicles 112
Company Meeting 112
Videoconference/Web Conference 113
Business TV 114
Conference Calls 115
Print Piece/Letter 116
Newsletters 117
E-mail 118
Intranet 119
One on One 121
Bulletin Boards 122
Unusual Means of Sharing 122
And Now a Word about PowerPoint 123
Ready, Set, No Not Yet 125

6. A MATCH, A ZIPPO, OR A BLOWTORCH   127

Step 6: Choose Your Champions   127
   Where to Find a Champion   128
   Getting Champions on Board   128
Step 7: Now, Execute the Plan   132
   Do I Have to Eat All My Carrots?   133
   So What's First?   134
Step 8: Measure and Adapt   135
   What Are the Ways to Measure?   136
   Planning Tools for Measurement   137
Principles of Good Marketing   140
   The Need for Alignment   140
   Be Persistent and Consistent   141
   Simple Sells   142
   Is There Such a Thing as Too Much Communication?   144
   Just One Thing   145
   Is Everyone Pulling in the Same Direction?   146

7. TRAINING AS A MARKETING TOOL   147

How Can Companies Use Training as a Marketing Tool?   148
Grow, Develop, and Satisfy Employees   148
   What's In It for Me?   149
   Cross-Training and Test-Driving New Roles   151
   Missed Opportunities   151
   Coaching   153
   Mentoring   154
Getting Everyone on the Same Page   155
   Orientation: The Message Starts Here   155
   Skills Training and Company Philosophy Equal a Happy Union   158
   Train as Though Every Employee Is a Corporate Representative   160
The Change Experience: Gaining Their Buy-In   161
Some Other Things to Keep in Mind   162
   Evaluate Your Training for Effectiveness   163
   Use Experiential Learning   166
   Market Your Training Internally and Externally   166
   Build a Social Network for Your Employees through Training   167
   Use Employees as Trainers   168
   Make Training Fun!   169

8. **D2D** *The Sum Is Greater than the Parts*   171
   Cinderella Finds Her Glass Slipper   172
   Branding Before Branding Was Cool   174
   Benefits of Marketing Your Department   177
   And Now the Dark Side   178

9. **TORCHBEARERS** *Rewards and Recognition*   181
   The Rules of Rewards and Recognition   182
   Reinforcement: The Framework   183
       Whom Are You Recognizing?   184
       Will You Focus on Measurable Criteria and/or Subjective Factors?   184
       How Will You Communicate Your Selection Criteria?   185
       How Will You Accept Employee Submissions?   185
       Who Will Decide the Winner?   185
       How Often Will You Recognize/Reward?   186
   A Different Kind of Recognition   186
   Other Factors to Consider   188
       Recognize Specific Behaviors to Reinforce Your Company's Vision   189
   The Big Question: What's the Reward?   190
       PDAs: Public Displays of Appreciation Are Essential   190
   Beyond the Trophy   191
       Brand Smart: Take Advantage of Your Industry   193
       Sharing Ownership   196
       Overcoming Obstacles   197
       Recognizing the Greater Good   199

10. **TRUE LIFE SITUATIONS**   203
    A Midsize Merger   204
    Hook, Line, and Sinker   207
    You Have to Crack Some Eggs   210
    Two Organizations Save a Penny, Spend a Million   212
    Don't Be a Fireless Leader   214

APPENDIX   217
BIBLIOGRAPHY   245
INDEX   247

Preface

The year 1966 was a newsworthy year. Walt Disney died. Twenty-year-old Oriole pitcher Jim Palmer pitched a complete-game shutout in the World Series. The United States bombed North Vietnam. President Lyndon Baines Johnson signed the Freedom of Information Act, giving the media access to government records. Historian and author Arthur Schlesinger, speechwriter and special assistant to President John F. Kennedy, won the Pulitzer Prize for *A Thousand Days,* describing Kennedy's short-lived presidency. The Supreme Court's Miranda decision required that defendants be informed of their rights. Frank Sinatra, 50, married Mia Farrow, 21. And the Beatles' John Lennon proclaimed: "We [the Beatles] are more popular than Jesus."

That same year, I enrolled in the journalism school at Loyola University in New Orleans. Fraught with political intrigues, legal shenanigans, an unpopular war, and important films like *A Man for All Seasons,* 1966 was a supremely serious year. It was also a heady time to be studying the news.

As future journalists, we revered news icon Walter Cronkite and tried to emulate the responsible voice of the *Washington Post.* We learned legal terms like *prurient interest,* used at the time to define obscenity. And I wrote a term paper on the role of the media in uncovering Senator Joe McCarthy's "commie" witch hunt of the 1950s. I'm sure we took ourselves much too seriously, but we felt honor-bound to uphold the principles of good, clean journalism. We were protecting freedom.

In January 1967, The Doors released "Light My Fire." In a sense, it was an anthem for those of us who were fueled by our passion for our profession.

Twelve years and a slice of reality later, I had a journalism degree but never had had a real job. Unfortunately, I was divorcing and needed money. So I swallowed my self-righteous, syrupy-sweet journalistic pride and looked for a job to pay the rent. Well, wouldn't you know it, I landed in the lowest form of writing: corporate public relations. According to the journalist's bible (no doubt written by John Peter Zenger and printed on the Gutenberg press), this was approximately equal to torturing small animals.

For the first year of my corporate career, I felt like a heel. I edited the weekly newsletter and wrote things that, in my mind, represented something short of the truth. I was ashamed, but I was also excited to be earning a paycheck.

Soon, I began to understand that I could use public relations (aka communications or internal communications) for "good" instead of "evil." I learned that my job was not to cram corporate pabulum down employees' throats, but rather to help them understand the company's business. By sharing information about financial goals, benefits programs, or new processes, I could contribute to the well-being of the company as well as employees.

By 1986, the 20th anniversary of my matriculation at Loyola, I started my own communications company. I was now even lower than a PR hack; I was a *consultant*. Scott Adams, the father of the Dilbert comic strip, has made a good living depicting the pitfalls of poor management and the inept consultants who exacerbate their problems. And I could see myself in Ratbert, the stereotypical consultant in the Dilbert strip.

Yet I had high ideals, dreams of helping corporations achieve their goals through communication. I had clients from a variety of companies in a variety of industries, but I noticed a pattern: the issues were pretty much the same from one to the next. And most could be dramatically improved by communication. Simply by getting people to share what they knew, I could help a manufacturing company improve its productivity and reduce accidents, get restaurant managers to encourage employees to take advantage of their benefits, and overcome polarization in a financial institution group by helping managers and employees understand each other's concerns. I now viewed my job as something other than spin doctor. I was an upstanding member of society, contributing to economic growth and greater understanding among people.

As an independent contractor, I was able to shed the corporate labels of PR and corporate communications. In 1993, I changed my business card to read, "Spellbinders, Inc.—Internal and External Marketing."

Here's the long and short of internal marketing: Employees must buy your message before your customers do. They must understand why your product or service is important, know what it can do for customers, believe in its integrity, and be inspired to make it even better. Employees have to understand where the company is headed and why. And they must be treated as grown-ups who can handle the truth, even when it's unpleasant. They have to be dedicated to working together to build the business. And finally, they should feel proud to tell people what they do and where they work. When they feel like that, everyone will know it—especially your customers.

I live in Memphis, Tennessee, headquarters of FedEx. If you want to find people who fit the description I just gave you, you only have to bump into one of the thousands of fanatic FedEx employees who live here. Or ask the tellers at First Horizon National, a company regularly named among the 100 Best Places to Work. Hampton Inn and Homewood Suites by Hilton hotels have a combined workforce of about 50,000. And it's hard to find anyone who thinks his or her brand is anything but number one.

These companies have this in common: Their leaders understand that employees play a crucial role in their success, and they're willing to put their words into action.

When we perform public relations/communications/internal marketing, it's not a loosey-goosey love-in kind of thing. We use the same scientific process as we do for external marketing. We identify key target audiences. We dissect the population into groups, such as managers, line-level employees, senior management, and so on. We take time to understand their needs, and we tell them what they need to know in the way they can best understand and use the information. We "sell" to them, so that they can feel proud of their company's strengths and can genuinely endorse their products to customers.

Are we still spin doctors? No, we aren't. Do we position information? Yes, we do. But we do it in a way that merely contributes to understanding. We don't lie about a company's strategies or stretch the truth to trick employees. We *do* try to lead companies away from a paternalistic attitude, suggesting instead that they trust employees to know the truth. We listen to the internal audiences' concerns and suggestions and validate them by recommending ways management can address significant issues that, left untended, may sink the mother ship. And finally, we help departments market themselves within the company, helping them build relationships to encourage awareness and respect for what they do.

Now here's our big secret: You don't have to be a consultant to do internal marketing. A team leader at any level can do it. A department head can do it. One group in a company can do it with the audiences it relates to. If you're alive, breathing, and have a message you want someone to hear and support, you can do internal marketing. Yes, it's a process. Yes, it should be a cradle-to-grave endeavor. But if you do it—really do it and mean it—you will have the most motivated and dedicated employees on earth.

Perhaps today my journalism professors and fellow students would frown on my willingness to dip my pen in poison corporate ink. So be it. When I see companies and employees thriving in a cooperative, mutually beneficial relationship, I give the J-school purists a nod and move to my next assignment. Good companies everywhere need to learn how to better engage and motivate their employees, to build pride in their organizations, and to create an environment where people feel good about their jobs. It's good for the company, it's good for employees, and it's good for customers. So come on, baby, light their fire.

Susan Drake, 2005

Acknowledgments

To all the people who lit our fire . . .

Our agent, Sheree Bykofsky, Janet Rosen, and the team; Michael Cunningham, Jack Kiburz, and the team at Dearborn Trade Publishing; Phil Cordell, who brought the three of us together; and Mark Kaestner, who made it Hampton.

Thanks to all who contributed their intellect and support to this endeavor: Susan Gross, Jim Holthouser, Michael Wilson, Jeff King, Bill Fromm, Phyllis Huang, Joerg Schumann, Mike Hill, Rhonni Vazquez and Alex Hermann from IBM, Jim Koch and Michelle Sullivan from Boston Beer Company, Gary Cortell and Amber Milt from *BusinessWeek TV,* Curt Welling from Americares, Richard Berman from Manhattanville College, Steve Mariotti from NFTE, Bill Jacobs, formerly from Mastercard, John Simon and Barrie Kessler from SoundExchange, Glyn Lobo from Dechert LLP, Seth Goldman from Honest Tea, and Jim Rogers. Special thanks to Vic Sarjoo for his incredible support and generosity. If you ever need anything for any reason, no matter how unreasonable, Vic is your man.

Thank you Ben and Jerry for helping us get through the book.

About the Authors

Susan M. Drake is the founder and president of Spellbinders, Inc., an 18-year-old internal and external marketing and communications consultancy. She and her associates are dedicated to the proposition that you can have fun while making clients' lives easier and their businesses more profitable. The hallmark of Spellbinders is nonconformist solutions that absolutely work. (http://www.spellbindersinc.com)

Michelle J. Gulman is a writer, speaker, and entrepreneur who provides management consulting solutions to *Fortune* 500 companies in her spare time. She is an expert at practicing internal marketing on herself whenever she is shopping. She usually lives out of a suitcase, but does her dry cleaning in New York City.

Sara M. Roberts is the founder and principal of Roberts Golden Consulting (http://www.robertsgolden.com) based in San Francisco, California. Roberts Golden provides best-in-class consulting services in the areas of internal marketing, organizational change management, and large-scale communication and training strategy and implementation.

Her background includes experience within a big-five consulting firm as well as internal consulting positions within major corporations. She has led many projects to enhance employee performance and gain buy-in at all levels. (E-mail: sara@robertsgolden.com)

For more tips, resources, and funny stories, and to learn more about the authors, please visit http://www.lighttheirfire.com.

The time to hesitate is through . . .
JIM MORRISON

Chapter 1

THE HOT TOPIC OF INTERNAL MARKETING

If Ben Franklin hadn't taken his baseball coach's advice, he probably wouldn't have discovered what he called "electric fire," and we might all still be in the dark.

Few people know that among Franklin's many interests was a great love of baseball. In fact, he almost certainly would have had an illustrious career as a pitcher for the Philadelphia Patriots if he had had the right kind of encouragement, recognition, and training. Unfortunately, he couldn't control his curve ball, and his coach and teammates didn't offer him any tips or coaching, or even a kind word, that might have helped him improve his game.

Franklin's baseball career came to an abrupt end during the 1751 World Series playoffs. The Philadelphia Patriots were up against the Washington Turncoats. The bases were loaded and Benedict Arnold was up to bat. The sky turned ominous as the thunderheads gathered. Franklin wiped the sweat from his brow and adjusted his wig. Arnold pulled his red coat tighter around him and dug his boot in the sand. Franklin wound up for the pitch.

"Ball!" the umpire shouted as the ball kicked up dirt at Arnold's feet. In the bleachers, the crowd was booing. He wound up for the second pitch.

"Ball!" Another bad curve ball whizzed past Arnold's left ear. That was close. If only his coach had given him some pointers, Ben thought. Maybe if he had told him a bit about the competition so he would have a competitive advantage—anything! After all, as he liked to say, an ounce of prevention was worth a pound of cure. Just a bit of guidance ahead of time and he wouldn't be in this predicament. You know, united we stand, divided we fall. He hiked up his pantaloons and wound up once more.

This time, Franklin decided to try a straight fastball, but he was so nervous that he flung it right at Arnold's head. Benedict Arnold went down with a thud, and Franklin thought to himself that Arnold would do well to retire to a quiet life of professional lawn tennis. He looked despondently on as a revived Arnold and the rest of the Turncoats on the bases walked to a 13-0 victory.

His coach, who of course had never offered a single good piece of advice about baseball, gave Franklin the best advice of his life as he fired him that day. "Benjamin Franklin," he thundered, "Go fly a kite!"

· · · · ·

Okay, so we made that story up.

We tell it, however, to illustrate the incredible power of simple things, like communication, encouragement, recognition, and training—simple things that make up what has become known as "internal marketing."

All of us will recognize a former (or maybe current) boss in Franklin's coach, and you may be thinking to yourself, "Boy, I know how that feels. I try to do the best job I can, but my company just doesn't give me all the information, training and, encouragement I need." Or, you may be wondering, "Was baseball even invented in 1751?" It wasn't. We looked it up.

Think about this: How has your company shaped *your* life? If you're a leader in your company, think about the enormous influence you have on your employees. You have the ability to light a fire in your employees and let your company shine with their light, or you can douse the flame by not giving them the right resources and tools to make them successful.

Internal marketing can help you create motivated employees through practicing four "E" behaviors: energizing, enabling, and empowering your team members, and ensuring that they achieve objectives and are recognized and rewarded for their accomplishments. Ben Franklin might have said that you're creating "electric fire" in their bellies. We say you're getting them just plain fired up about your company—*their* company. Using the techniques in this book, you will learn how to create an "E" or exceptional culture that will energize your employees, enhance teamwork, and motivate performance that will always wow your customers. Voilà! E-employees.

WHAT IS INTERNAL MARKETING?

Internal marketing involves getting employees to love your brand so they, in turn, will convince customers to love it. But don't employees automatically love their company and its brand? Frankly, no, they don't. It doesn't mean the company is bad. It could mean the company lacks personality and passion. Face it, some people simply do their jobs and draw a paycheck. There's nothing wrong with that. Such performance is acceptable, but it's definitely not desirable. An employee who is ho-hum about your company's brand or product is going to do a ho-hum job and give ho-hum service to customers. Ho-hum service leads to lost business.

Conversely, an employee who is fired up will make it obvious to coworkers and customers that he loves it. Translation: You will too.

By using proven marketing techniques, you can increase employees' buy-in to your company's ideas, values, and initiatives. In a sense, you "sell" your brand's "promise" to employees.

What is a brand promise? It's the essence of what you say you'll deliver to customers. It's a delicious burger, a low-cost appliance, a bra that accomplishes wonders, a hassle-free travel experience, or a truck that attracts beautiful women and won't get stuck in the mud.

"E" employees carry out the promise. They make sure they cook the burger to perfection, point out the appliance's cost-saving features, make travel arrangements correctly, and build a reliable truck. As for the bra? You're on your own with that one.

Promises, Promises

Jeff King, president of the Atlanta office of Barkley Evergreen & Partners Inc., believes that internal marketing, done right, is fundamentally the most important component of building a successful brand. Barkley Evergreen & Partners Inc., is one of the nation's top ten independently owned advertising and marketing firms, with offices in Atlanta and Kansas City.

"Internal marketing is so critical. Its role is to *make sure that brand promises are kept*. Marketing and ad agency people are great at dreaming up compelling promises but it's up to the employees to keep those promises," says Jeff.

It's rare that employees live a business philosophy all the way from the factory to the sales floor, from the back office to the customer service desk, from the president's office to the drive-through window. It's rare, but it's also possible. And it's no accident. Dedicated employees magically emerge in companies that are built on relationships, not rules.

Jeff has spent his entire career helping clients find unique and relevant ways to communicate their brand messages to their consumers, but he understands first and foremost that if employees don't understand the brand promise—or, worse yet, are not in agreement with it—then the promise will fall short. "We can make great ads all day long, but if consumers have bad experiences with the brand, it's all for naught," he says. "With effective internal marketing, your external marketing efforts are much more likely to succeed."

TRUE LOVE OR LIP SERVICE?

Companies that consider their employees to be their greatest assets are the ones that ultimately prevail. Once again, all together, let's repeat that sentence aloud for effect. Companies that consider their employees to be their greatest assets are the ones that ultimately prevail.

What does that statement actually mean? Many companies say they're employee-centric and put employees first. "Hip, hip, hurray for our employees!" they say through their perpetual mantra, "The employees at our company are the number one key to our success!"

Unfortunately, the declarations are often just lip service. How can you tell? Ask the employees. They'll explain the reality of how they're being treated. They can correctly interpret what it means when management lays them off without first considering other cost-cutting measures; or when they're not receiving forthright and honest communications, if any at all; or when management keeps information so close to the vest that employees are nervous and distrustful. In the absence of information, the grapevine fills the vacuum with lies and half-truths. Employees begin to feel that the company doesn't have a smidgeon of loyalty to them for all they've contributed to the "relationship." When management takes the credit and employees take the blame, it's a formula for disaster.

These actions by management send a message to employees—a very negative message. It could be different.

We know all too well that companies spend millions of dollars each year on marketing their products to potential customers. Why do they spend so little on marketing to the people who need to love them the most—their employees?

Some companies understand that they must get employees to buy in before the customers will buy. These are the companies that have begun to put together the blueprint for a long-lasting and successful business.

Two Ways to Sell the Promise

There are two types of internal marketing:

1. An ongoing process of sharing information and recognizing employees' contributions
2. A short-term, specific initiative that helps achieve a particular goal

An ongoing process is the foundation for a healthy culture where employees operate by the "one for all and all for the customer" philosophy. Continuous internal marketing is the solid foundation on which to build a world-class organization.

Short-term internal marketing initiatives help you do things like implement a new program, adapt to change, overcome adversity, survive a merger, and so on. A little later we'll describe to you a situation in which FedEx headed off a pilots' strike using internal marketing tools.

First, let's look at an ongoing, culture-changing internal marketing effort.

From Train Wreck to Triple Crown

"I would walk in front of a truck for him if he asked me to," said Adrian Sugars, a director at Homewood Suites by Hilton hotels. She was referring to her boss, Jim Holthouser, the brand leader. Few stories illustrate the power of internal marketing the way this one does.

Five years ago, Jim was looking for a few good men and women to help him revive a languishing hotel brand. He had just taken the reins of Homewood, a brand that comprised about 80 hotels.

Homewood was born in 1989 of a consumer need for a hotel that caters to travelers staying more than five nights. Positioned as an "extended stay" hotel, the Homewood concept was perfectly timed and priced for the market. It featured a fully equipped kitchen and other amenities that appealed to travelers on extended visits. From all indications, it was a sure bet. Yet ten years later, growth was stalled. The brand had been stifled by several factors. First, the industry in general was overdeveloped so money was hard to come by. Second, the public had no real understanding of why they should stay at a Homewood rather than a traditional hotel. Third, the brand lacked direction. Fourth, consumers were uninformed of the brand's features. Even employees in other Hilton Hotels Corporation (HHC) business units gave little thought to it. It became, "Oh yeah, Homewood. Is it still around?"

Jim had a challenge.

While he had a huge consumer marketing opportunity on his hands, there was also a bear of a development hurdle. From day one, he knew that an equally important part of his strategy must be to differentiate the brand not just outside HHC, but inside as well.

"We needed really smart people to help us grow," says Jim. "But when I first got to Homewood, I would post a job and wouldn't get a single candidate. People gravitate to business units that are cool and going places, but inside our corporation our brand was all but invisible. I did a lot of drumbeating to get people to sit up and take notice. We had to create brand excitement internally so we could get our share of the talent at HHC."

Personality shines through. "We've been tireless in developing and promoting Homewood's personality," he says. "We're informal, irreverent, not political, and lots of fun. We say thank you a *lot*. We offer great training, development, and recognition. And we do a ton of communication so that everyone on our team stays absolutely focused on extended stay. Our team members are proud of our brand, and they want guests to love it as well. When a guest walks in the door, team members make sure that this experience will be unforgettable. We make the guest part of the Homewood family too."

He's not from Dallas, but Jim is a cheerleader of the first order. And he doesn't spend a lot of money on uniforms and pompons. He does have a vice president of brand performance and sales, Bill Duncan, and a vice president of marketing, Calvin Stovall, who share his rah-rah mentality. Together they've implemented regular group conference calls with field-based corporate team members and regular progress updates via conference calls with every general manager. Jim sends written thank-you notes and makes congratulatory calls to team members who have excelled. They've created a special designation for their top directors of sales entitling them to a weeklong, fun training session at headquarters. The bonding that takes place during those few days leaves each participant feeling that she's a truly important part of a sales commando team—with heart.

All the world's a stage. Each year, the Homewood brand hosts an annual conference for hotel owners, general managers, and directors of sales from all the Homewood properties. The meeting features speeches from the top three guys, but it deviates from the typical corporate formula of boring speeches and charts. These three share themselves generously with the group, letting their personalities show through.

Calvin, by far the most outrageous of the three, each year has upped the energy of his entrance and his big finish. Several years ago he began his "run" with a speech worthy of a big-tent evangelist, midway tearing his shirt open to reveal a big Superman-style "S." By the end of the "revival," the audience members were on their feet. The next year, he made his point about never resting on your laurels by dancing along to one-hit wonders including "I'm Too Sexy" (for my shirt) and "Mickey" (you're so fine you blow my mind). In 2004, he made his grand entrance playing drum major to an all-girl high school drum line. He was bigger and louder than life.

Bill, the one with a sense of humor as dry as the Sahara, takes the role of the guy who gets no respect. "Gee, thanks," he whines. "Why do I always have to follow Calvin?"

And Jim? He took a personal risk when he gave a virtuoso performance on a grand piano. His message: No matter what you're doing, you have to play with passion.

You may never have seen people cry at an annual corporate conference, but we have.

On the big stage, as well as on many small stages throughout the year, these three exude love for Homewood and the team members. By sharing a part of themselves, they have endeared themselves to their constituents and established a unique personality for their brand. Homewood, after all, is a place where people are treated like friends.

Scary as it may seem in a business setting, letting others see the vulnerable, fun side of you is a way to build stronger relationships. People relate to people, not to stuffed corporate shirts.

The result of this "whole lotta love" is that Homewood's team shows a whole lot of love to hotel guests. And guests return the favor.

Winning in the long run. Jim says, "In 2004, we won what I call the triple crown: three top industry awards based on consumers' positive opinions. Those awards are a direct result of a culture where team members fanatically carry out our brand promise." Homewood employees now have the information they need to do a great job, but more than that, they go above and beyond to serve guests because they own the brand's success.

"I've always known that internal marketing is just as important as external marketing and my experience here validates my belief," says Jim. Perhaps most telling of what internal marketing can do are the feelings of team members like Adrian Sugars. (Despite her offer, Jim doesn't generally ask her to face off with a truck.)

After five years, Jim no longer has a recruiting problem. "Now when we post a job, we have more candidates than we can handle." In an industry where turnover is one of the biggest challenges, Homewood retains its high performers. Jim no longer has a system growth problem either. The brand is enjoying a major acceleration in development. And the payoff doesn't stop there, because effective internal marketing continues to build momentum.

He's grateful for the turnaround. Says Jim, "Some people call that leadership. I call it selling."

As you think about how you might conduct an internal marketing campaign, maybe you're a bit put off at the idea of a Superman outfit or a marching band. Maybe you're not flamboyant or at all comfortable creating a corporate pep rally. Not everyone can play concert piano or get a laugh with a meaningful pause. But read on. Every leader develops his or her own style, a way to reach employees in a way that feels right. We'll show you other, more traditional ways to "get your groove on," gain supporters, and engender brand love.

Think it's worth a shot?

The Flip Side

Sometimes internal marketing becomes essential when companies face adversity. Consider Intel's struggles in 2004. Serious product delivery delays and recalls began the downward spiral. When the stock price dropped by one-third over six months, it threatened to derail the company's ability to survive.

To avert disaster, CEO Craig Barrett explained that the executives were "revisiting the meaning of Intel culture and talking about management expectations, and starting to put in place the indicators, reviews, and management attention to start to turn these problems around."

Dan Hutcheson, analyst at VLSI Research, said, "It's not an issue of blame. It's really an issue of getting everybody marching to the same beat."

Perhaps a strong internal marketing campaign could have prevented, or at least ameliorated, some of the problems. In any case, it became a must-have when the company hit its low point.

Too bad Intel had to suffer such serious losses. Ask Barrett and I'll bet he'd say that compared with the cost of problems, internal marketing would have been a lot cheaper.

IT STARTS WITH CULTURE

Culture is a reflection of a company's leadership, philosophy, history, and shared beliefs and values. A company's culture inevitably affects whether employees will support or hinder desired change; it drives behavior. However, misalignment within a company's culture can cause employees to be resistant and slow to change. They may even sabotage desired behaviors. Internal marketing communicates a vision of the company culture, strengthens an already powerful brand culture, and gives employees a road map for action.

We've seen how Homewood Suites has created a strong culture of warm relationships with team members and with guests. Hewlett-Packard is another company that has been very purposeful in creating a healthy culture for itself. It's the "HP Way." Its corporate culture is based on respect for others, a sense of community, and plain hard work. It has been meticulous in ensuring that its culture is grown and cultivated through extensive employee and management training that supports the company's values.

Carly Fiorina, the current CEO of Hewlett-Packard, has been quoted as saying, "In this new world, we must always remember that technology is only as valuable as the use to which it is put. In the end, technology is ultimately about people."

What this means to me personally, as a consumer, is that every printer I've owned since 1986 has been a Hewlett-Packard. Considering I've only owned three models in 18 years, I'd say that's pretty good quality, wouldn't you?

It's Still about Walking the Talk

When management lives and communicates the culture every day, two very important things happen:

1. Employees see that management adheres to the company's stated beliefs, also known as "walking the talk."
2. It proves that management believes employees to be the heart and soul of the company.

How many times have you seen this disconnect: A company touts teamwork as an important part of company culture but rewards people based on individual performance? Or a company says that creativity and innovation are core values, but then it penalizes risk-takers?

If companies don't practice what they preach, employees become distrustful and confused. But if the culture is reinforced every day through appropriate modeling, training, and communication, employees become role models too.

A Tale of Two Organizations

I have seen firsthand how important a strong culture is in companies that want their employees to support and live the brand. I was working within a large communications company, in which two large technology organizations were in the midst of a massive corporate restructure. The restructure had to do with the way they did business—everything from how they managed projects, to how they would hand off to other departments, to how they would practice new behaviors such as enhanced communication and interpersonal skills.

I had the role of working with both of the organizations' leaders to "institutionalize" the changes that were taking place. Mick J., leader of Group 1, constantly communicated with employees about the road map, shared a poignant and compelling vision of success, and always remembered that line-level employees were the ones making him look good.

The employees of Mick's group were referred to internally as "mavericks with fiery, entrepreneurial spirits." Management gave them the autonomy to problem-solve. Many were chartered to help create the vision and collectively reengineer the processes for the new organization. Like any group in transition, it had growing pains due to the massive changes taking place. But the group stuck together, united by its common vision and shared involvement, and it emerged a stronger, more cohesive group as a result.

The second organization was run by three or four different persons within the period of a year. Management couldn't even get an executive to stay with the organization for more than a few months. "Well, if management isn't committed, why should I stay?" wondered employees. From their point of view, this was just about as bad as it gets!

Elvis P., the newest leader of dysfunctional Group 2, hired nearly 40 external consultants to create the new organization and decide which processes it would use in the future. Thus, he unwittingly sent out the message to employees that they could not be trusted to undertake an important task such as leading the initiative to create and shape their own organization, despite the fact that the changes would affect the production of products most of them had worked on their entire careers. *Leadership had an opportunity to endorse and grow an employee-focused culture but did not.*

Not surprisingly, Elvis's organization—a group of nearly 4,000 people—hated coming to work every day. People would grumble and mock the consultants' "new behavior of the week."

Group 2's new structure and processes fell apart shortly after the consultants left. How could it not, with 4,000 people stubbornly resisting the change, and undoubtedly communicating their unhappiness to friends, family, and (uh-oh) customers?

The organization still struggles to this day to keep its employees motivated and inspired.

THE "E" FACTOR

The purpose of internal marketing is to create "E" employees, people whose passion for what they do erases the boundaries of service. They no longer think about their jobs as a set of specific tasks. Instead, their work involves whatever it takes to contribute to the well-being of the company.

Recently we were in Chicago to speak about internal branding at a conference. The day before the presentation, a manicure was in order. The hotel concierge informed me that there was an Elizabeth Arden spa across the street. I'd never been to an Elizabeth Arden facility, but I had a positive perception of the brand. I couldn't wait to see firsthand what sort of luxury awaited me behind The Red Door.

The service was truly exceptional. Then, midway through my manicure, I heard someone say, "Hey, I smell smoke." Not exactly what someone wants to hear when she's on the fourth floor of a high rise with wet fingernails. We calmly evacuated the building, gathering outside the entrance to await clearance or to forfeit our luxury treatment.

I actually felt quite lucky. Some of the customers were in a considerably less-enviable predicament. One woman, having been in the middle of a massage, hugged a bathrobe around herself. Another, with aluminum foil and bleach in her hair, was in danger of becoming a Donatella Versace look-alike.

Because the building was being renovated, there was a waist-high stack of lumber at the curb. My manicurist, who left the building without her purse but *with* her manicure implements, suggested I take a seat on the lumber. She would finish my manicure. On the sidewalk. In Chicago.

What impression do you suppose I have now of Elizabeth Arden? That fire scare could have been quite an annoying experience. Instead, it became great dinnertime conversation. One employee who put my needs first cemented my favorable feelings about The Red Door. Her name is Luda, and she's an "E" employee.

Here's another "E" employee story.

A truck driver was transporting a load of cows across the country. Although he would normally sleep in his 18-wheeler, he had a problem on this trip: The cows were mooing so much he couldn't sleep. He saw a Hampton Inn hotel and checked in for a quiet night's sleep. At some point, he explained to a hotel team member that the cows just wouldn't shut up. He had fed them, watered them, and didn't know what more to do.

Because he was in the heartland of America, the truck driver was fortunate to meet a Hampton breakfast hostess who knew just a bit about cows. She informed him that the poor cows needed milking. But he was a truck driver. He didn't know one end of a cow from the other. Not to worry. The breakfast hostess went outside and milked the cows.

We all know that this person's job description certainly didn't include milking cows. But that was an unimportant detail to her. She understood that her job was to take care of guests.

Because the leader of the Hampton brand, Phil Cordell, is a super communicator, he repeated this story every chance he got. As a result, that hostess is a symbol of service at Hampton Inn. She's an "E" employee.

"E" employees:

- Take risks
- Make suggestions
- Support others
- Smile a lot
- Motivate their coworkers
- Enjoy work
- Attract trust
- Like customers
- Define service as whatever the customer needs (whether it's an external customer buying the product or an internal customer who needs assistance with a project)

An "E" employee is someone you'd like to see at the window of a Wendy's drive-through, holding your baby in the newborn nursery, tuning up your car, installing your smoke detectors, designing your financial plan, doing an intake on your sick kitty, and cleaning your soiled Armani suit.

"E" employees would make great best friends.

HOW DO YOU CREATE AN "E" ENVIRONMENT?

Energizing a team doesn't mean instituting aerobics to get people more pumped up. So then what are the ways to ignite your employees' passion? To create inspired and motivated employees who perform well and deliver on your brand promise, consider the four "E" factors:

1. Engage
2. Enable
3. Empower
4. Ensure

Internal marketing is the channel by which you can accomplish the four "E" factors.

How to Engage

Ever been completely nose-down in a good book and can't put it aside? You know that feeling. You're sleep-deprived, you have a million things to accomplish tomorrow, and yet you're up at 3:00 AM and can't bear to put that darned book down. Why on earth would anyone do that to themselves? In my case, it's because I'm completely engaged in the story. I want to find out more. I'm excited and on the edge of my seat. Now, just as a good book engages the reader, companies can engage employees. How do you do this? Tell your story!

Involve employees in helping you create your company's vision and then paint a clear and vivid picture of how you want them to execute it. Sure, you should give them the facts of the matter, objectives and such. But your story is more than facts. It's a description of the heart and soul of your brand. It's what makes your brand different, special, wonderful, and valued by customers and employees alike. Craft your story with all the quirky parts included, and fill it with humor and warmth.

The late Kemmons Wilson founded Holiday Inn hotels in 1952. The man is a PR person's dream. I would wager big money that any person who ever worked at the company could tell the Holiday Inn brand story. How hard can it be when it is this colorful:

- Kemmons's career began when he owned a popcorn machine.
- When he invented his hotel product, he named it after a Bing Crosby movie.
- He put the company's name on the towels as an advertising trick, figuring if people "borrowed" them others would learn of Holiday Inn.

- He picked out hotel sites by flying around in a prop plane and looking down for locations.
- He wrote notes to the HR department on cocktail napkins with messages such as, "Hire this guy."

This is the folklore, the color commentary, the fascinating stuff that gives a company a heart and its leader a bigger-than-life personality.

In 1990, a large British ale brewer and pub owner, Bass, bought Holiday Inns and moved the company's headquarters from Memphis to Atlanta. The move hastened the departure of a number of lifelong employees who chose to remain in Memphis. Not to be denied the camaraderie they so enjoyed when they worked at Holiday Inns, the former employees organized a reunion. Each year, hundreds of people—yes, hundreds—would get together at a Holiday Inn hotel and regale each other with old stories and family photos. In the early days of the reunions, attendees included the founder himself, the original company "chaplain on call," and the woman who was the longest-term employee. That reunion has been held every year for 14 years, and the stories are just as amusing now as they have been for the more than 50 years the company has been around.

Kemmons generated a wealth of yarn to weave a pretty colorful quilt. But even if your founder isn't a character, your company is bound to have an interesting heritage.

Just keep talking. Steve Jobs, CEO and founder of Apple, is another person with an amazing talent for sharing a clearly defined story and cause. He articulates to employees what Apple stands for and where it's headed, and he gives employees something to believe in. His ability to succinctly get his vision across is undoubtedly one of the reasons that Apple is a "cult brand" and an inspiration to many of its employees and customers.

Another methodical communicator emerged several years ago at Sprint. He was respected by his employees, a group of 30 people, for being an ideal communicator. Each year, he sat down to build his communication strategy and plan for the upcoming year. He spent a lot of time and effort making sure that he did not let communication with his group slip through the cracks. Inevitably, things in his organization, just as in yours, changed from day to day; however, he still created an overall internal communication plan that considered the key messages for the year as well as the best communication vehicles to get the message across.

He planned his themes and key messages for his monthly staff meetings ahead of time, basing his topics on issues employees expressed an interest in discussing. After all, the most interesting thing you can talk about is what someone wants to hear.

No matter how big or small your organization is, it's important to thoughtfully plan how you will communicate. Good relationships aren't built accidentally.

Feeling a part of something big. Another way to engage employees is to build and sustain a sense of community. When you do this, employees believe "we're all in this together" and that they are part of something "larger than themselves." This sense of belonging is at the top of the list of employee needs. When you create a community, people feel a sense of responsibility and obligation to support each other. Larger companies can train management to create this sense of community within each individual department so that the organization as a whole is speaking with "one voice."

How to Enable

Companies can do right by their employees by creating a supportive environment along with tools and direction. You've already engaged them, showing them a vision of an ideal company. Now help them understand that they have the power to make that vision a reality.

What are some ways to create such an environment? Solid companies have processes and procedures that describe what's expected of employees; but they also know that rules are used for the purpose of guidance.

What you are trying to avoid is an employee who says to a customer or a coworker:

- That's not how we do it.
- That's not our policy.
- It's not my job.
- I don't have the authority to do that.

Here's a funny story that happened some years ago. A couple was visiting Springfield, Missouri, and happened to visit a rather famous outdoors equipment store. In the clothing area, the woman saw a pair of sunglasses in a display case. They called her name. She asked the clerk where she might find an identical pair on the sales floor, and the clerk directed her downstairs to the sunglasses department.

These weren't just any sunglasses, I assure you. These were *the* sunglasses. The woman searched the extensive collection of eye apparel, but no match was to be found.

She returned to the clothing area upstairs and asked the clerk if she could please get the pair of glasses from the display case. The answer: "I'm not allowed to do that."

By now, this had become a matter of principle. The woman asked for the manager. The manager wasn't on duty. She insisted that if they didn't take the damn display apart, she would do it herself. After about 30 minutes of haggling, the employees finally opened the case and gave her the glasses. But there was no price on them.

"We can't sell these to you without a price," she was told.

"How about if I go downstairs and find the most expensive pair of glasses, and pay whatever that price is?" said the woman.

"Oh no, we can't do that. We can only sell them to you if we have a price."

Well, the story goes on, and, believe it or not, customer persistence finally won out, but why all the hassle? By the time it was over, both the customer and the employee were exhausted from the exchange.

Management's job is to remove roadblocks and obstacles—to get rid of stupid procedures that annoy customers and make the employee's work a chore. If this employee had worked for a company that enabled him, he would have satisfied the customer without having to jump over so many hurdles, and without the fear of being reprimanded for doing his job.

Training enables action. I'm sure you'll agree it's important that employees have the skills and knowledge they need to be successful. After all, it's a two-sided equation: If we ask employees to improve their performance or take on a new way of doing work, we must give them first-class training and every opportunity to become peak performers.

Training takes many forms—skill-based, job-specific, performance improvement. It might be done in workshops or seminars, on the job, or in one-on-one coaching sessions. The important thing about training is that it takes place over the full course of an employee's career with you. We'll talk more specifically about training in Chapter 7.

Besides formal training, one of the best enablers is a good work environment. It's actually a critical factor in getting people to care about and love their jobs. One environmental factor you can control, at least to some degree, is the frustration of office politics. Do not take part in negative discussions or design manipulative plans to get even or steal power. It will typically come back to bite you. Employees remember that you've grumbled along with them and then they lose respect for you as a person who can make things happen.

Earn trust and respect by being an optimist. And, by the way, don't be afraid to have some fun at work! We all need to have some time out once in a while. I have worked in multiple environments and the ones that are the most motivating to me are the relaxed ones where I have felt empowered to do my work without constant supervision. Employees need to be praised in meaningful ways, not only in performance reviews but also on the spot, preferably in front of others. Praise in public, coach in private.

And whether you're an executive, manager, or employee, remind yourself each day to take some time to pat someone on the back, whether it's someone who works with you or yourself.

> *"I praise loudly. I blame softly."*
> **CATHERINE THE GREAT, 1729–1796**

How to Empower

Great companies provide the autonomy and platform for employees to do what it takes to do their jobs well. These companies encourage "out of the box" thinking and individual problem solving.

> *"We cannot solve our problems with the same
> level of thinking that created them."*
> **ALBERT EINSTEIN**

Employees are empowered to make the right decisions, especially when they directly serve the customer. Give people permission to make mistakes. Let them know what outcome you want, but avoid telling them how to get there. As long as the result is what you want, allow employees the flexibility to do it their way.

Get this: Every employee in every position at nearly 1,300 Hampton Inn hotels has the power to invoke "100% Hampton," the brand's 100 percent unconditional satisfaction service guarantee. If, for any reason, a guest of their hotel is dissatisfied with their stay, the employee can give them one night's stay, free of charge. No need to get manager approval!

Whoa! Now isn't that risky? No, it isn't. The company estimates that for every dollar it gives away, it gets about seven dollars back in repeat business. Employees don't just go around irresponsibly exercising this power. They think and act like owners of the business. They take ownership, pride, and a responsible approach. They sometimes even milk cows.

In focus groups Hampton conducted in 2002 concerning its guarantee, employees were asked if they thought the guarantee was still important. They said, "Absolutely!" They say that the guarantee creates the culture of service of which they feel so proud.

Another way you can empower employees is to encourage lots of risk taking and involve them at all levels of decision making. Remember the example of the organizations run by Mick and Elvis? Mick knew that involving employees in the direction and vision process (normally reserved for just executives) really motivated and inspired his organization to work hard for him and for the company.

Are you empowering your employees? Can your employees truthfully and resoundingly respond yes to these statements?

- I am actively encouraged to volunteer new ideas and make suggestions for the improvement of our company.
- I feel my company takes my suggestions and ideas into consideration.
- I feel I can freely express my opinions even if I know others in my company may disagree.
- My management generally lets me decide the most appropriate way for me to get my work done.

How to Ensure

Ensuring means measuring success and providing clear guidance. It's also about demanding accountability at all levels and then giving appropriate rewards and recognition for performance.

It works the same at all levels. Senior people must be accountable for how well they're communicating a clear vision and developing the careers of those who work for them, just as line-level employees are responsible for developing products or providing good customer service.

Ensuring or enforcing doesn't mean wielding a big stick when it comes to job descriptions and formal policies and processes. However, creating an energized workforce does not mean that employees have free rein to do whatever they wish. It means they have a sense of where they're going. When they reach their goal, they're doing 100 percent, and they're entitled to recognition. When they don't reach their goal, it's not time for punishment. It's time for reestablishing goals, coaching for performance, training when necessary, and then measuring again.

Challenge people but don't subject them to excessive demands. Frustration won't motivate, it will discourage. If employees make mistakes, guide them.

Accountability to yourself and your employees is so important. It's easier when you make public commitments about initiatives and actions. I ran my first (and so far my only) marathon a few years ago. I'm sure the sole reason that I was actually able to do it was because I made a public declaration to my friends and family that I would finish! Promises said out loud have more impact.

The same is true of companies. Announce your project goals so that everyone knows them and can encourage their coworkers. Keep people informed of progress so the goals stay front of mind. Celebrate interim successes, or make a course correction immediately if something is not working. Waiting to tell people what's going on until it's too late increases the chances the rumor mill will run rampant!

HOW DO EMPLOYEES CONTRIBUTE TO ACCOMPLISHING BUSINESS GOALS?

By now you've seen a few examples of the role that motivated employees play in satisfying customers and how uncommitted employees undermine performance. Here's a clear-cut example of how two companies in the same industry had dramatically different outcomes.

Bill Fromm, a nationally known expert in strategic planning and customer service, created the marketing firm Barkley Evergreen & Partners. Because he saw a need for internal marketing, he cofounded the Service Management Group. Bill's client roster represents companies involved in retail, fast food, business-to-business services, franchise operations, telecommunications products, and the automotive aftermarket. *Inc.* magazine's Regional Entrepreneur of the Year in 1995, Bill is the author of *The Ten Commandments of Business and How To Break Them* and *The Real Heroes of Business and Not a CEO Among Them*. Bill has appeared on television on *Today* and *The Oprah Winfrey Show* and was featured on a segment produced by CBS's *48 Hours* about customer service.

"We're in the midst of a case study in this country on the airline industry," says Bill. "Southwest is the most profitable airline in the entire world. How is it that they've never lost a dime and made more money than all the other airlines combined? It's because the employees love the company and people love the airline. It's that simple. Their employees are awesome and it translates into hard and concrete business results. I was sitting on an Eastern Airlines plane before they went out of business and an airline attendant had a button with their president's name on it with an "X" slashed through it. That, I knew, was the death rattle of the company—when a company's employees are telling you how screwed up they are."

We would never suggest that these companies' internal marketing—or lack thereof—totally defined their financial performance.

But we believe quite firmly that the link between employee morale and financial outcomes is quite evident in these examples.

Consider this equation:

Brand promise + Companies' ability to deliver = Business results

Back in the days when we transported goods by mule and wagon, we put our success in the hands (that is, hooves) of the mule. If the mule went lame, or just didn't want to pull the wagon, the goods didn't arrive.

Who carries the brand promise to your customers? Employees. So it's nearly a certainty that if your employees aren't equipped or inspired to deliver your brand promise, your customers won't receive it. The bottom line is that you won't achieve the business results you want.

Not every employee is in direct contact with the customer, but every single one of them contributes. Let's face it. They all talk to each other and all form opinions of how well or poorly management is doing. To illustrate how inspired and motivated employees translate into the success of business goals, consider the following data from an article in the June 2001 issue of *Adweek*.

- Forty-nine percent of consumers make a point of *not* buying certain brands or services when they shop.
- Eighty-one percent of those respondents attributed their reason to a bad personal experience with the brand or its representatives.

Every single one of your employees represents your brand. From the product development folks to the marketing folks to the customer call centers, every single employee has the power to make or break your brand over time.

We're certainly not implying that you need to have 100 percent of your employees on board to have a successful company. It's unrealistic to think that everyone will be out blowing the happy trumpet. Apply the 80/20 principle here. The best practice is to focus your efforts on the 80 percent who support you or are willing to be convinced. Don't worry so much about trying to convert or pacify people who are the loudest squawkers that you forget about the 80 percent who are on the right track. Seek to understand why the 20 percent is unhappy or unmotivated but don't focus all of your efforts on them. If you do, those who are on board may begin to waver and doubt that you have their best interests in mind.

DO YOU NEED INTERNAL MARKETING?

Are your employees excited to come to work every day? Does your team seem motivated? Do you have low turnover? Do you get the cooperation you'd like from other departments? Does management understand and support your projects from a financial perspective? Does every one of your team members claim responsibility for serving your customers? And, perhaps most important, would any of your company's employees say they'd walk in front of a truck for you or your top managers?

If you answered no to any of these questions, this book is a good investment for you.

Let's face it. Most companies need internal marketing. Many organizations have the gift of taking committed, enthusiastic people and turning them into cynics over time. Inevitably, this leads to failed initiatives, grandiose plans, and restructures that have either disappeared or failed.

You know that you need internal marketing when employee turnover is high, change abounds, and you must clearly and succinctly articulate the vision and goals to your employees.

What If Yours Is Not a Big Corporation?

Does a small company need internal marketing?

Meet Michael Wilson. Michael is the general manager of a 64-room Hampton Inn hotel in Jonesville/Elkin, North Carolina. The closest "big city" is Winston-Salem, population 185,776. The nearest airport is 65 miles away.

In the years 2002 and 2003, this hotel was the number one hotel in the entire Hampton system. That's number one out of about 1,250 properties. In 2001, it was number two. In 2000, it was number three. In fact, for the last seven years, Michael's hotel has been one of the top five hotels in the Hampton system. Its year-end occupancy has been 90 percent in an industry where normal occupancy ranges from 65 percent to 75 percent.

We were conducting focus groups with general managers of high-ranking hotels to hear their ideas about employee motivation. During the session Michael said, "I don't understand why more owners don't do internal marketing. They spend a lot on marketing to customers, but not to their employees.

"The main thing I want to emphasize is that if you can sell your property to your employees, then you can sell your property to anyone. Employees become more excited and energized," he says. "I get to know the employee a bit. Ask them about their family. If you treat them like family, then they will look forward to coming to work. The way I know that an employee is enjoying their job is when they lose track of time and say, 'The day just flew by.'"

In the case of this hotel, the owner does practice internal marketing. Michael says, "Our owners will go to the supervisors of each department to see what they need to make their jobs easier. They also ask the supervisors for ways that they can assist in rewarding employees."

"The Christmas party that the owners throw is a very big deal to the employees. The employees receive tickets in their payroll checks. Trips, DVD players, color TVs, and stereos are given away at the party. Everyone walks away with some sort of prize or gift. Also, all employees get a Christmas bonus, which is usually a gift card to a local grocery store. They used to give away turkeys and hams, but employees said they would rather be able to choose their own groceries and Christmas meals."

Isn't that a bit much for such a small enterprise to give away color TVs and trips? Before you answer, let us tell you a few things that have happened at his hotel:

- *Employees go the extra mile.* Recently a front desk employee heard that a guest was having car trouble. He followed her to the service station and then brought her back to the hotel. Would an "average" employee do that?
- *Guests talk.* Much of the hotel's business results from word-of-mouth advertising, particularly from the older guests.
- *Employees stay.* It's not like Michael has a huge job pool from which to choose. The entire population of Jonesville/Elkin is 6,366. But it's not a problem for him because his employees tend to stick around. "Employees really like working here because there's a good bit of flexibility. In fact, I have more part-time employees than full-time. The more people you have, the more you can work around their schedules and give them the hours they like."
- *Employees connect with guests.* The breakfast hostess exchanges recipes with guests. "They look at it like it's *their kitchen.* Atmosphere is everything!"

"I want the employees to have fun, because if they're having fun, it rubs off on the guests," says Michael.

This company puts a lot of effort into internal marketing, which leads to a lot of good results. Large or small, every company needs team members who fanatically believe in what their company stands for, have a burning desire to share their company's story, and feel an intense satisfaction in seeing that they've contributed to the company's success. Create a culture, energize your team, and motivate performance. Once you do that, you're solid gold in your employees' hearts and your customers' minds.

Chapter

2

WHY LIGHT THEIR FIRE?

The Benefits of Internal Marketing

On November 17, 1998, 3,500 FedEx employees stormed FedEx headquarters in Memphis, Tennessee. They carried picket signs and posters, along with an undeniable passion for their cause. They waved pompons and balloons and held up signs that read: Absolutely, Positively, Without a Doubt, Lock 'Em Out!

They weren't on strike against FedEx. They were rallying in support of FedEx. The pilot union had threatened to go on strike, an action that would have debilitated FedEx during the critical holiday shopping season. (The express shipping division processes 3.1 million packages on a normal day.) Employees wanted the pilots—and FedEx management—to know that they were 100 percent behind FedEx. They wanted management to know that they would still do "absolutely, positively" whatever it will take to deliver to their customers.

That's the story that hit the papers the next morning, and that's what FedEx customers, shareholders, and the pilots read. But there's a story behind this story.

It's true that the employees took it upon themselves to gather in support. They weren't told or even asked to rally in defense of the company. But FedEx *did* do something—and, more importantly, it had been doing something all along—that made the blood run purple through the veins of FedEx employees.

That "something" was internal marketing.

As rumblings of the strike surfaced at FedEx headquarters, their teams sprung into action. FedEx partnered with its PR firm, Ketchum, to define an internal marketing strategy specifically for the potential strike. In FedEx's long-standing tradition of honest and inspirational communication, they reached out to employees. Internal marketing was something FedEx was very comfortable with; it had long been a core part of an ongoing strategy to build employee loyalty and passion. Judging by employees' reactions to the strike, it's also something FedEx did very well.

One of the most serious threats was employees' fear of losing their jobs. The campaign was launched to reassure the nonpilot employee population through consistent, comprehensive communications. The "Absolutely, Positively, Whatever It Takes" theme helped keep employees focused on customer needs and reinforced a positive environment. All across FedEx headquarters you could see the campaign theme on posters, buttons, banners, bumper stickers, T-shirts, and sweatshirts. The company used its digital broadcast network, FXTV, as well as a special intranet "sitelet."

The FedEx CEO and COO conducted 15 meetings with 6,000 employees in Memphis and Indianapolis—the company's two largest operations. The digital TV coverage was broadcast globally.

Now the big question: Did the campaign work? Can internal marketing really help build employee loyalty and lead to a stronger, more successful company? The answer is "absolutely, positively" yes!

Here are highlights of the company's remarkable results:

- Incredibly, FedEx's stock price actually soared during the strike negotiations, to the amazement of investors and the

delight of shareholders. This was due in part to two factors: the rally staged by employees and a marketing campaign directed at two other audiences—shareholders and analysts.
- During the negotiations, FedEx internal service measurements were the highest in the company's history. An overwhelming number of employees demonstrated their "purple blood" loyalty via e-mails and letters to the editor of *The Commercial Appeal* in Memphis.
- Just weeks after the internal marketing campaign was launched, the union postponed job action, went back to the negotiating table, and overwhelmingly approved an industry-leading contract. FedEx was saved from a potentially devastating strike.
- The following year when Fortune magazine again ranked FedEx in its "Top 100 To Work For" list, it cited the rally and said, "There's good reason for such loyalty."

FIRE THAT GIVES LIFE: WHY INTERNAL MARKETING IS CRUCIAL TO BUSINESS PERFORMANCE

Internal marketing can save the day in a crisis, as it did for FedEx, but more often, such employee engagement and loyalty shows up day in and day out in small but powerful acts of service.

Keep in mind that internal marketing is a long-term strategy. It's about creating a deep, genuine connection with employees. It's not something a company can pull out of a hat and expect employees to buy into overnight.

FedEx's campaign for the pilot strike succeeded mostly because it further reinforced the good internal marketing practices that FedEx had been enacting for many years. Employees already had a sense of loyalty when FedEx implemented its targeted campaign, so when the company appealed to them, employees wanted to return the favor. These are the types of things that have a sustainable impact on business performance.

Internal marketing has been directly linked to employee satisfaction, which in turn is linked to customer satisfaction, which is, of course, linked to superior business performance. Internal marketing also improves a company's bottom line on the other side of the balance sheet.

Increasing employee retention rates:

- Saves the company the cost of hiring and training new talent
- Boosts employees' individual contributions
- Allows a company to realize and exceed the value of employee salaries

The benefits of internal marketing follow this pattern:

1. Internal marketing creates "E" employees.
2. "E" employees are loyal employees.
3. "E" employees perform.
4. "E" employees wow customers.
5. The sum of the parts is extraordinary.

INTERNAL MARKETING CREATES "E" EMPLOYEES

Employees who are engaged in their jobs and their company's mission, enabled to do their jobs well, and empowered to succeed are happier than employees who are not. That's common sense. But sometimes researchers need to validate common sense. Mercer Consulting conducted a study comparing employee satisfaction with internal marketing practices such as corporate communications and business literacy. It arrived at some interesting, if not surprising, results.

Here's what it found in a 2002 study:

- Employees who felt that their organization "does a good job of keeping employees informed about matters that affect them" were almost *three times less likely to leave* than those who felt their company did not communicate well.
- Seven times as many employees reported being "dissatisfied" at work when they felt their companies did a poor job of communicating.
- Employees who felt enabled in their jobs were far less likely to be dissatisfied with and contemplate leaving their company, by 39 percent and 30 percent respectively, compared with employees who didn't feel enabled.
- Over eight times as many employees who did not feel empowered "with the information and assistance required to manage their careers" were dissatisfied compared with those who did feel empowered.

Interestingly, not being paid fairly was the least important of the factors that contributed to employees being dissatisfied and wanting to leave. Only 36 percent of employees who felt they were "not paid fairly given [their] performance and contribution to [their] organization" contemplated leaving.

Curtis R. Welling, CEO of AmeriCares, said to us, "Being successful financially is a necessary condition for corporate success, but it isn't a sufficient condition to *stay* successful. Money only has certain staying power. If you don't do more for your employees, you are vulnerable. Unless you've established an emotional, not just financial, connection with your employees, you'll always be susceptible to the next person who can trump you by one dollar. "

It's true. In business as well as in romance, you just can't buy love.

CAN'T BUY ME LOVE: IT TAKES MORE THAN PAY TO MAKE PEOPLE STAY

"The current method of motivating employees involves frightening them until their arteries harden, then trying to make it all better by giving them inexpensive gifts bearing the company logo."
SCOTT ADAMS, THE DILBERT FUTURE

The dedication and loyalty we're talking about can't be bought. It's a given that employees should be compensated fairly. That's one of the ways a company shows its employees that it values and respects them. But financial compensation is only the beginning. If you don't create an emotional connection with your employees, you can open your wallet wide and it won't make a difference.

Amber Milt had been working part time at a major production company for three years and was totally fed up. She says her experience there was absolutely unbearable. Never had she felt so unappreciated. "They made me feel completely disposable and worthless. I never got a single thank you for anything I did."

At the same time, she was freelancing for *BusinessWeek TV*. The contrast between the two companies was mind blowing. *BusinessWeek TV*'s executive producer and co-owner, Gary Cortell, sat Amber down when she first joined as a freelancer and told her, "Anything you want to do here, I will help you do, to the best of my ability." And he would end up keeping that promise. Amber reveled in the respect, open communication, and genuine caring she received from the *BusinessWeek TV* management and staff.

One Friday, Gary offered her a full-time editor position at *BusinessWeek TV*. Amber was thrilled.

The following Monday, completely by coincidence, the big production studio called and also offered her a full-time position, "for a lot more money," she recalls. She considered the credentials that would accrue. The studio was a leader in the industry and to be an editor there would have turbo-boosted her career. "I made the decision instantly, though. No amount of money is worth feeling unappreciated. You can't put a monetary value on your own self-worth . . . I was burned out." A year into her new job at *BusinessWeek TV,* Amber was still in touch with people from the big production company. It had not managed to fill the position it offered her. "The turnover rate there is about six months," she said.

BURNOUT: THE EXPENSIVE COST OF NOT MARKETING TO EMPLOYEES

Employees like Amber who aren't engaged, enabled, and empowered at their company will eventually figure out that they can go somewhere else. That's great news if yours is the company that gains a superstar like Amber, and it's really bad news if yours is the company that loses her. Not only do you lose a great talent, you also lose money. The cost of employee turnover is staggering.

A Gallup Poll estimates:

- For a line-level position, it costs 0.41 times the annual salary to find, hire, and train a new employee.
- For a professional associate position, it costs 1.77 times salary.
- For management positions, it costs a whopping 2.44 times salary.

"For an organization of 10,000 employees," Gallup authors Curt Coffman and Gabriel Gonzalez-Molina write, "a 5 percent decrease in employee turnover saves $4 million for front-line employees earning $20,000 a year, $35 million for professional associates earning $40,000 a year, and $97 million for managers earning $80,000 a year."

For our happy, fictitious 10,000-employee company, that's a total savings of $136 million per year just by reducing the turnover rate by 5 percent. As we said, we recognize the value of financially rewarding employees for their work. So you can guess what we recommend you do with some of that extra money.

What can you do to have numbers like these in your favor? Internal marketing can help prevent employees from leaving your company by eliminating these common employee feelings:

- "The company doesn't care about me." When companies don't bother to keep employees well informed, it sends a deadly message: We don't care about you and your contribution. Employees need to feel valued and cared for, which a company can do by communicating honestly with them (see Chapter 5), rewarding and recognizing their efforts, and giving them growth opportunities (see Chapter 7).
- "I didn't feel that I was really making a difference." Mike Hill has seen people come and go at IBM for over 25 years, and he knows that, "When people leave, they don't leave because of the money. They leave because they don't feel like they've made a difference." People want to feel that they contribute to the company's success, or at least their team's success. Involve your employees in the vision and mission of the company, try to incorporate employee feedback and involvement in decision-making processes, and make sure you communicate the value of their roles within the organization. IBM's "Jam" sessions (see Chapter 5) are superb examples of involving all employees in strategic decision making—a true accomplishment for an organization 330,000 people strong.
- "I'm not proud of what I do." We all associate ourselves with our jobs to some extent and our self-esteem demands that we're proud of the company we work for, the job we do, and the contribution we make. Help employees feel good about all of these through honest, authentic communications, rewards, and recognition. Chapter 9 has some suggestions.
- "I'm not growing." If employees don't feel they have the opportunity to grow their skills and to position themselves for success, they're not likely to stick around. This is one of the reasons we believe training is an important internal marketing tool. Offer your employees options to grow personally

and professionally at your company and they will be grateful. If your training budget is tight, there are several creative ways to allow people to enhance their skills at hardly any cost. Check out Chapter 7 for some economical ideas.

FIRED UP: THE ENORMOUS VALUE OF HIGH PERFORMANCE

The benefits of marketing to your employees are numerous. If you succeed in reaching them at an emotional level, not only will they stay, but they will perform for you in ways that will astound you. Pride is motivating. Being well-informed and well-trained enables people to do more, and high performance can be contagious and set new standards across the company.

Following are just a few more ways you'll benefit from effective internal marketing.

"E" Employees Earn Their Keep

There's a big difference in the value and productivity of an employee who is engaged, enabled, and empowered and one who isn't. The Gallup Poll we referred to earlier found that disengaged employees cost on average one-third of an employee's salary in lost productivity, compared to engaged employees. That means that an employee earning $30,000 per year costs the company $10,200 in lost productivity. A $50,000 per year employee costs $17,000. For disengaged management, the cost is staggering. Forty-two independent Gallup surveys show that 75 percent of all employees at most companies are not engaged at any given time. Do the math for a 10,000-person company and you'll see hundreds of millions of dollars per year going up in smoke.

"E" Employees Go Beyond the Call of Duty

It really was *BusinessWeek TV*'s gain and the major production company's loss when Amber Milt chose the emotional connection over the big bucks. Amber feels a sense of personal pride in her work because of Gary's business philosophy. She often works late nights to perfect a show and to support her coworkers. Shortly after she joined, on her own initiative and mostly on her own time, she completely redesigned the look of the show and took it to a new level. "It's not my show, it's Gary's show. But I would do anything for him. I believe in what I do and take pride in the product as though it's mine." Gary Cortell treats his employees as family; he trusts them, offers them whatever they need, and gives them a long leash. In exchange, he expects his "family" to make him proud, and they are only too happy to do that in return for all he does for them.

Fewer People Can Do More

SoundExchange, a nonprofit digital media company in Washington, D.C., enjoys many benefits from the open, friendly culture that its internal marketing programs have helped create. Not only does the company have very low turnover (only two people have voluntarily departed over the past four years) but it also has kept its employees so motivated and passionate about the company and its growth potential, that employees are happy to step up to bat. "We promote people from within the company," says Barrie Kessler, SoundExchange's COO, "because they really want to take on more and more challenging roles." This has allowed SoundExchange to grow significantly in its membership and revenues while keeping approximately the same number of employees over the last four years—that's a huge advantage, especially for a nonprofit company that carefully watches its costs.

"E" Employees Raise the Performance of an Entire Group

Even one person's pride and motivation will shine at your company, but watch what happens when an entire group—and even the entire company—works in unison toward shared goals.

In the mid-1990s, MasterCard International had grown into an unwieldy organization that was divided along management lines. Petty wars and lack of communication between departments were hurting business, and Bill Jacobs, senior executive VP of global resources, watched as MasterCard International fell further behind the competition. Jacobs and then-CEO Gene Lockhart made the decision to develop a program called TEAM (Team Excellence at MasterCard). Through the program, 10 to 15 employees at a time went offsite for a week to build cross-departmental relationships and help individuals work more effectively. "The program was so effective because it was rolled out worldwide to every single employee," says Jacobs.

The program took several years to fully roll out, and it came with an expensive price tag, but the results were worth it. "The walls started coming down," said Jacobs. "People were talking to each other. Before the program, the finance department and the marketing department didn't see eye to eye, but when you throw people together for a week, they start to open up and realize they have more in common than they thought."

The program was a "major building block" in the company's improved performance over the next several years. Ultimately, it helped MasterCard International eclipse its number one competitor, Visa U.S.A.

The massive internal marketing initiative also sent a powerful message to MasterCard International employees: We will invest time and money to put everyone through the program because we're committed to helping employees work more effectively. Everyone is important and contributes to MasterCard International's success.

Combine all these factors, and you'll see an incredible difference in personal and business performance when people feel involved and valued. It's an important leadership lesson for us all.

A Miserable Success

Vic Sarjoo was only 23 when he took over the presidency of a chapter of the Boys & Girls Clubs of America. An extremely self-driven, motivated person, Vic also had his own financial advisory firm under his belt. But as a one-person band, he didn't have any leadership experience. Suddenly he found himself in charge of a large organization whose board members had 20 years' more experience than he did. Without any formal training to draw on, he simply applied the principles that had brought him success in the past.

He was, at least by some measures, very successful: In less than two years, he doubled the club's budget and staff and raised a million dollars for the club—more than the club had raised in the last ten years combined. The problem was he was flying solo. He completely cut his own staff and board members out of his activities as president. "I really didn't even recognize the board or the staff," he says. "I thought I was faster and smarter and I could do it alone."

True, he succeeded alone, but the success was empty. "If you look back at my presidency, they were the most successful years the club had ever had, financially. But I'm not remembered well," Vic says. "I lost their trust." Vic resigned from the club and the door pretty much hit him on the way out.

We've all seen this kind of leadership—the "do as I say or I'll do it myself" leadership style. Most of us are guilty of having done it ourselves at one time or another. It seems quicker and more efficient, and when the stakes are high and the needs are urgent, it feels safer to just do it ourselves.

That kind of leadership doesn't build genuine, sustainable success, though. The key to being an effective leader is to create other leaders— "E" employees—all around you. The mantra of internal marketing could be "sell it, don't tell it." When we involve people in our success, and appeal to them on an emotional level, rather than by force, the results may not be as quick and efficient at first, but the success is built on a solid foundation that will get you through the hardest times.

When Those Who Are Led Lead

When people learn a lesson the hard way, they often learn it well. Vic went on to lead another nonprofit organization, a chapter of the Future Business Leaders of America (FBLA), and this time he got it right. "A nonprofit with a 100-year history [like the Boys & Girls Clubs] should have been much easier to sell," he said, "and now here I was, not much more than a kid myself, trying to get disadvantaged, inner-city youth in front of senior leadership of major corporations."

Despite his youth, he did it. "I applied the right principles this time," he said. "I wanted to get these kids to work together as a team without directly leading them." Vic realized that he needed to communicate to the kids that he believed in them and that they really mattered. "I let them know that they could realize their goals and dreams, that they could make things happen in the world."

What resulted was that this group of inner-city youth established direct relationships with top executives at companies like CNN, MTV, ESPN, and Dechert Law. Several students landed corporate internships and jump-started their journeys to their own boardrooms. Their enthusiasm and performance soared. "It made such a powerful difference," he said, "when people felt empowered."

Vic has also learned to apply internal marketing practices in his own financial services business, VSAM Global Asset Management, where he now has a staff of employees who understand their value to VSAM's success and are empowered to help it succeed. "I let my staff know that I need them more than they need me." He also gives them a great deal of autonomy and responsibility, saying, "When they have some ownership they seem to protect it more."

One day Vic received a phone call from one of his FBLA students. "Vic," the voice said, "I'm on Wall Street. I'm knocking on doors. They won't let me in." Jason, a 17-year-old kid from the Bronx area, was standing outside the Wall Street offices of JP Morgan and other financial giants in a suit, carrying his resume, determined to get a job and be successful just like his role model. "A little bit of recognition inspires people to do heroic things," Vic laughs.

"E" EMPLOYEES WOW CUSTOMERS

Your employees *will* do heroic things for you. And even in a small company, loyalty and performance can translate into millions of dollars of increased profit per year. Best of all, these heroes will stay with you. Still, that only scratches the surface of the benefits you will reap if you engage, enable, and empower your employees.

Ultimately, the greatest value of internal marketing relates to satisfied customers.

"E" Employees Wow Your Customers

The levels of service that "E" employees deliver will blow away your customers and your competition. The greatest differentiator a company can achieve is its reputation—its brand—for phenomenal service, superior products and quality in everything it does. And that kind of a brand is built on the shoulders of "E" employees.

FedEx management focuses on internal marketing because they understand that their "E" employees will deliver fantastic service, wow their customers, and turn tremendous profits. They named their corporate philosophy after a concept called PSP—people, service, profits, in that order.

Richard Branson, CEO of Virgin, swears by the same philosophy, which is why he's able to take one industry after another by storm. "We give top priorities to the interests of our staff; second priority to those of our customers; third to shareholders," says Branson. "This is not only a reflection of the importance of our people, it is also the most positive way of fitting together these three priorities. Working backwards, the interests of our shareholders depend upon high levels of customer satisfaction . . . which depends on high standards of service from our people, which depends on happy staff who are proud of the company they work for."

Bill Marriott, CEO of Marriott, follows in the footsteps of his father, who also understood the way to build a successful company. "My father believed very strongly that if people were happy in their work they would take good care of the customer, and the customer would come back again and again. He believed that, and he made it happen. He had tremendous loyalty to our employees, and I think we still do."

The fact is that the more reliable, genuine, and sustainable way to be successful for the long haul really is to treat your employees like your most valuable customers. Give them the inspiration, the resources, and the power to deliver the best service your customers have ever seen.

Here are some of the ways "E" employees will wow customers:

- Engaged employees are passionate about the company and their work, and this comes through in every customer interaction, every product and service, and the quality of everything they do. At the end of the day, a company doesn't take care of its customers—employees do. That's true for every business in the world.
- Enabled employees have the resources and information to provide better customer service, deliver higher quality prod-

ucts and services, and help the company grow. Being enabled imbues employees with the responsibility and accountability to be successful.
- Empowered employees have a sense of ownership that makes them extremely passionate about their work. They also have the freedom to provide the highest level of service for customers. Remember the 100 percent Hampton guarantee?

In the words of a nursery rhyme, "When they're good, they're very, very good. . . ."

And When They're Not, They're Horrid

How would you feel if we told you that we're all just one or two sentences away from disaster?

Few employers would suspect that in about 30 seconds one employee can undo all the advertising, product improvements, technological advances, and good will the company has worked so hard to develop. Unless you've got employees on board, you're sitting naked in a snowstorm. You could probably regale us with plenty of your own stories of poor service, but indulge us as we share two examples of how employees can undermine your success.

This first story comes from Clearwater, Florida. A resort hotel there has a pool and spa area that requires a pass code for entrance. A guest went to the front desk to ask for the code. The front desk person referred the guest to the spa staff.

When the guest approached the spa employee with her question, the spa employee told her she should check with the front desk. Once the guest explained that she had already been to the front desk and was referred to the spa, the spa employee said: "Oh, they always get everything wrong. They can't even get the basics right."

How could a *resort* hotel with a *spa* operate with such poor service? What exactly is their mission, and why do employees not know it? If employees do know, why aren't they living it? Could internal marketing have helped? It certainly could.

- It could have taught that employee the true meaning of customer service.
- It could have helped both the front desk and the spa employees understand the specifics of the pass code procedure.
- It could have taught the front desk person that it's best to walk a person to her destination, or ask someone else to accompany the guest if they are unable to leave their post.
- It could create a universal understanding among employees that they should never, never talk negatively about another employee or department.

Why can Ritz-Carlton operate with impeccable service, yet this resort cannot? Because Ritz-Carlton knows how to create a service culture that permeates its properties. And you can, too.

Let's switch gears now and move to a hospital setting.

We were asked to spend several days with a new client evaluating its customer satisfaction. When we do that, we take into account many factors, some of which never make a customer satisfaction survey. One criterion is how welcome we feel when we arrive at the facility. Is the appearance warm and welcoming, or is it cold, stark, messy, dirty, and so on? The arrival quality also covers signage, and whether it clearly tells us what we need to know. If there is an employee at a reception desk, how does that person greet us?

We try to put ourselves in the shoes of the customer. Come with us and imagine that you're a person about to be admitted for a procedure. We'll be your family members. You don't feel well and you are anxious about being in the hospital. Perhaps you're about to have a diagnostic test to determine if you have a very serious illness. In this particular situation, we enter through a parking garage that goes directly into the building. The only person we encounter is a security guard, who gets on the elevator with us. We both say good morning and ask how he's doing. With a foul attitude, he replies, "Surviving."

Do you feel better now that you've been greeted by a hospital employee? Yikes. His demeanor was bad enough, but think about his choice of words. Surviving? Considering that this is a hospital, his choice of words did not exactly exhibit sensitivity.

Yes, it really happened. And the next day, we separately encountered the guard. Not willing to be daunted by his nasty attitude, we persisted. When I again asked him, "And how are you doing today?" his response was, "Just surviving." When my partner said, "Well, hello again. And how are you doing today?" his answer was, "Still surviving. And if you ask me again a month from now, it will still be 'surviving.'"

Is there any chance that this could reflect favorably on the institution? Absolutely not. Is there any chance it will create an unfavorable impression? You bet. It only takes one encounter to taint the opinions of everyone on the receiving end of his negativity.

Thank goodness we were at the beginning of our assignment with this group. Management understands that there are areas for substantial improvement, and we're happy to help them achieve it.

THE SUM OF THE PARTS IS EXTRAORDINARY

The sum of all the benefits of internal marketing is something that is less tangible, but possibly of greater value than anything else a company can aspire to—a great brand.

A reputation in the market for having the greatest talent, treating your talent well, and delivering exceptional service and products is the most valuable asset. It's the most difficult quality to achieve and the most difficult quality for competitors to imitate.

It's impossible to duplicate a FedEx, a Virgin, or a Southwest Airlines. They are leaders in their industries because their employees say so. Their brands are powerful because every person on board works to that end. Much of that brand power, directly and indirectly, comes from each company's relationship with its employees.

The sum total of a company's relationship with its employees—the foundation of a great external brand and the result of a great internal marketing strategy—is also known as a company's internal brand.

Chapter 3

BRAND POWER

Creating an Internal Brand

Steve Jobs and Steve "The Woz" Wozniak created the first wood-encased Apple computer in their garages in 1976. Jobs hocked his Volkswagen van and the Woz sold his HP calculator to provide the up-front capital. They sold their first model for $666.66.

Despite modest beginnings, Jobs never thought of Apple as anything but a legend, and he never treated the people who worked for him as anything less, either. Steve Jobs wasn't making computers; he was changing the world.

By 1980, Apple was the largest personal computer maker in the world. Even today, with less than 4 percent of the personal computer market, Apple still wields an awesome and disproportionate power.

You might say the reason for Apple's powerful position is its brand, and you'd be right. Apple still has one of the most recognized brands and one of the most dedicated followings in the world. A brand like that is corporate nirvana. CEOs would sell the Armani suits off their backs to create a brand like Apple.

A legendary brand can withstand devastating shocks—the loss of its visionary leader, his return 15 years later, failure of several key products, erosion of most of its market share—and still emerge with card-carrying customers. Talk about cult status! Apple customers will happily take on a pack of hungry PC nerds to defend their beloved brand.

Yet the level of dedication of Apple customers pales in comparison with that of Apple employees. Apple employees are on a mission and they really do believe they're changing the world. (And they may not be entirely wrong.) It sort of redefines original sin—they live and die by everything Apple.

Could there be a correlation between employee devotion to Apple's brand and Apple's customer loyalty? *You bet.* Employees who believe in their brand create fervor and passion that shows in the products they create, the services they deliver, and the messages they convey to the rest of the world. It's like someone finally solved "the chicken or the egg" question. Employee brand loyalty creates customer brand loyalty, but at the end of the day, they're the same animal.

If your employees are sold on your company and its brand, selling your customers is a piece of apple pie. Apple may not have the biggest slice of the computer market anymore, but if there's one thing at which Apple excels, it's creating a tremendously powerful brand *within* its company. And that translates into one of the best-known and best-loved brands in the world. The advantage is priceless.

BEING A BEAUTIFUL BRAND

A great brand is like a pretty girl. People want her, they'll spend lots of money on her, and the world is her oyster. If you don't have a pretty brand, you can kiss your chances of customers chasing after you goodbye.

Everyone wants to have a beautiful brand, and to that end there are whole industries devoted to making your brand look good and sell well. They are the "cosmetic surgeons" of the corporate world. Experts collect billions of dollars a year for advertising, external marketing, and public relations aimed at dressing up brands and giving them a pretty image. They try to cover up the scandalous blemishes and highlight the company's best features. They add glam and glitter and play up a company's sex appeal as much as possible.

But at the end of the day, we all know the truth: a makeover only lasts a short time.

Sure, a company might be able to fool customers with a dazzling first impression, but sooner or later the façade will crack and the true nature of the company will be revealed. If it's not pretty on the inside, customers will never be attracted to it.

What makes a company naturally pretty? Companies that nurture themselves on the inside create a naturally beautiful exterior. Naturally pretty companies have good-looking *internal* brands. And how do you accomplish that? Why, through internal marketing, of course. Let us demonstrate.

First, let's evaluate what you're feeding your employees. If you're putting junk in, you're going to get junk out. Employees— your company's "body"—need proper nourishment, and in this case that means plenty of good communication. Introducing a variety of communication channels into your company's diet will keep the message interesting, and will make sure your body's getting all the essential information it needs.

What about exercise? Your company's body needs to be in good shape to meet everyday challenges as well as tough situations. Training allows your body to adapt to its environment more easily, and it keeps your company strong and capable of growth and innovation. Trust us, training will make your company glow!

Reward your company's body for its effort. Give it a big pat on the back and, may we recommend, a little treat once in a while (even splurge on a banana split—everything in moderation). Good self-esteem, after all, is the greatest beauty.

Look in the mirror. What do you see? If you're not making as much progress as you would like, try changing parts of your routine. Assessing and measuring your results is critical to your company's success.

Congratulations! Your company has a beautiful internal brand! Go ahead. If you've got it, flaunt it. *A beautiful company sells itself.*

PLAYING WITH MATCHES: HOW INTERNAL BRANDING LIGHTS THEIR FIRE

Having a beautiful internal brand is obviously pretty appealing in an aesthetic sense, but it also does more to contribute to your brand's health. There are four distinct ways your internal brand will help you go all the way:

1. *It will create awareness and consistency.* An internal brand heightens employees' awareness and understanding of your company's external brand, mission, and values, so they can communicate consistent and positive messages to the world.
2. *It will sustain a positive culture.* It reflects and sustains your company's unique culture and heritage.
3. *It will drive change.* It can help you deal with crises in a productive, positive way.
4. *It will attract and retain the best talent.* It can create an appealing and positive culture that everyone wants to be a part of, and no one wants to leave.

Create Awareness and Consistency

Your employees comprise one of your most powerful marketing forces. Whether you like it or not, your employees are already marketing your company, and they're either sending a positive or negative message.

Not long ago I was purchasing a toaster from a store in a mall. I intended to pay for it with a mall gift card I had received for Christmas. When I handed the card to the sales clerk, she groaned, "Oh, boy, I'm sorry." A somewhat ominous comment, wasn't it? Nevertheless, she attempted to process the card as payment. As she predicted, it didn't work.

The clerk followed up with a tirade about how lousy the cards are, and how they never work. As you might expect, I will never put a mall gift card under the Christmas tree for any of my friends or loved ones.

Like the sales clerk, if your own employees aren't sold on your brand then they won't sell your customers on the brand, either. Worse, if they're disgruntled and fed up with the company, their negative attitude will work against you to damage your brand image.

Employees broadcast messages about their company to the world around them. It's not just the front-line employees or those talking to your customers on the phone. Your employees in the finance department, HR, and IT impact the company's brand image and customer loyalty as well.

All employees have feelings about the company they work for, and they communicate their feelings in many ways, through many channels. Consider a few examples of the indirect ways your employees' lack of understanding and respect for your brand can sabotage customer loyalty:

- Employees communicate their opinions about the company in the quality of their work. Remember that employees who are disengaged at work provide one-third less value than those who are engaged.
- Employees communicate their feelings to their coworkers, family, friends, and, sometimes after a particularly stressful day, to anyone on the street who will listen. Many of those people may be your customers.

- Employees who don't understand your brand and its mission and values may send the wrong message or mixed messages about your brand to others, which can dilute your brand message and confuse customers.
- Employees who are unimpressed with your company and uninspired by your brand may leave, creating gaps in service, ramp-up time for new employees, and a price tag to replace them—all of which detracts from the ultimate goal of serving your customers. (Of course, if they are this disillusioned, you should be thankful they chose to leave.)

Sustain a Positive Culture

Richard Branson is such a superb marketer he's actually a brand unto himself in the corporate world. Virgin's intrepid CEO pulls sensationalist publicity stunts that constantly keep the Virgin name, and his own, in the press. What few people know is that Branson is also the consummate internal marketer. He has created a culture in each of his numerous companies in which all employees know that they are important to the company's success.

They also know Virgin's values very well because they're reminded of the values every day, and that helps Virgin sustain its superb culture. Virgin's values are present everywhere. Perhaps nowhere is this more evident than in management's actions and decision-making processes. The company considers new business based on whether the business will meet the criteria of the group's values. Because the new business has a key understanding of values straight from the beginning, everyone works toward the same end to communicate the brand personality. Another company famous for its culture is Southwest Airlines. There's a reason Southwest Airlines' ticker symbol is LUV: There's a whole lot of love going on between the company and its employees, and, in turn, between its employees and its customers. Southwest has one of the best reputations in the airline industry for genuinely friendly service, and that's proven to be a major competitive advantage.

Customers regularly ditch the elite status and perks they get from other airlines to travel the innovator of no-frills flying. Why? Because the service is outstanding. PR and external marketing alone can't create that LUV-ing feeling passengers get when they're on a Southwest flight (and it's certainly not the peanuts). Because Southwest does a fantastic job of marketing to its employees, it has created one of the strongest internal brands and cultures in the world—a culture of happy, loyal employees who want to treat their customers well. "People have come to visit Southwest Airlines saying they want to establish a culture similar to ours . . . and we tell them all we've done is just treat people right," says Southwest founder and chairman Herb Kelleher. Southwest is able to sustain its culture by constantly strengthening its internal brand through its core values.

Drive Change

Internal marketing is one of the most powerful tools at your disposal to effectively drive change inside your organization, and to deal with external changes that impact the company.

We've already seen an example of FedEx's use of internal marketing to help the company avoid the potential pilots' strike in 1998. Companies can use internal marketing campaigns to achieve both long-term and short-term specific goals, such as a change initiative, managing external change, coping with internal (and external) conflicts, and meeting short-term financial or other objectives.

Internal branding plays a critical role in the success of these kinds of initiatives. We use the same principles to brand an initiative that we use to create enthusiasm and commitment for a company's brand. But we have more flexibility with an initiative because each can have its own hallmark. An internal initiative's identity should be closely tied to the company's own brand and its mission and values, but it also should be distinct enough to evoke specific emotions and results.

When the three of us teamed up to help Hampton Inn hotels roll out a $100-million industry-leading initiative, we developed an extensive internal marketing plan and branded it "Make It Hampton." It was clean, catchy, and actionable, as well as easy to adapt to visuals, communications, and other branding devices. It integrated the company's existing branding and was a call to action, petitioning employees to help implement the elements that would move the brand to the next level. They were, indeed, "Making It Hampton."

Every communication, presentation, and plan, down to basic e-mails and memos, fully reinforced and strengthened the brand. By the time the project was officially launched at Hampton's annual conference in January 2004, every franchise owner, general manager, and corporate stakeholder was familiar with the Make It Hampton brand.

In the months before Make It Hampton's official launch, we also created another branded theme within the campaign. The theme was "One Voice," which honored the different "voices" that helped make the initiative a success. Beyond recognizing those who had contributed to the development of Make It Hampton, the goal of One Voice was to ensure that all the people who would represent the brand would be telling the same story, reinforcing the messages that were most important to management.

Phil Cordell, the senior VP of the Hampton brand, held monthly conference calls on the topic of the featured "voice" for that month. The calls were followed by weekly e-mails on the same topic, which included inspiring stories, facts and figures, quotes, and progress updates.

We used a one-page "brand story" picture as a training device to help team members understand Hampton's service culture, its position as a "lighthouse" brand, and how to connect with guests no matter what area of the hotel they worked in.

Hampton piloted the initiative with a select group of hotels that were targeted to be brand champions. Called "Frontrunners," the champions were given the opportunity to influence the direction of the initiative and were recognized and rewarded. This method organically created "positive rumors" throughout the organization.

One of the communication tools we used specifically for the champions was a newsletter called "The Front Line," which gave them progress updates, recognized them for their hard work and dedication, and told them how the initiative was being received by guests. The newsletter was just one of the special touches we gave the brand champions to make them feel special and create a positive view of the initiative and the brand as a whole. The brand champions participated in special meetings; were recognized with awards, gifts, and special parties; and were specifically honored at the official launch of Make It Hampton.

Attract and Retain the Best Talent

A strong internal brand brings many privileges, and not least among them is the power to attract and retain the best talent. When *Fortune* releases its list of 100 Best Companies to Work For, those companies get inundated with resumes before the ink on the magazine has dried.

Southwest Airlines is a perfect example of a company that benefits from its brand image from a recruiting standpoint. Over 90,000 hopeful candidates applied in 2001 for 3,600 available positions. There's even a story of one hopeful candidate who camped out with a sign that read: Will work for peanuts! And the loyalty is fierce. Southwest has one of the lowest attrition rates in the industry.

CREATING AN INTERNAL BRAND

Now the real fun begins—creating your internal brand. Will you be the next Nike? Coke? Gap? The blaze of the next great brand smolders in your eyes. You can see the spotlights, you eagerly anticipate the media attention. Britney Spears is dying to be in your next commercial. Tiger Woods is canceling his other advertising contracts to be your product's exclusive spokesperson. You're even picking out the color of your private jet.

Whoa there, hang on. Don't you already have a brand? You know, that little picture you see all over the place. That's a logo, isn't it? And you have a tagline, or a slogan, or a color scheme. You might even have an advertising jingle, mascot, or theme. Before you attempt to develop a new internal brand, what about your existing external brand? It's an established icon for your team.

You may not be creating a whole new brand, but is your internal brand the same thing as your external brand? Well, yes and no.

Remember that an internal brand serves many purposes, including creating a strong emotional tie with your company's mission and values—concepts that aren't necessarily advertised outside the company. It's okay, even advisable, to create an internal brand that is unique and distinct, but it should be strongly tied to your company's external brand. A unique internal brand allows you to target employee-specific messages that you wouldn't necessarily direct to your customers, and it can provide a sense of exclusivity to those messages. You may also define several unique and temporary internal branding campaigns for internal initiatives, which we'll talk about shortly.

That being said, more and more companies are designing holistic brands that are intended for multiple audiences, internal and external. We highly recommend this strategy because it guarantees that all your stakeholders will get the same, consistent brand images and core messages, while still allowing the flexibility to target messages to each group. You will find some internal branding campaign examples near the end of this chapter.

Be Persistent and Consistent

Every industry has its classic mantra. For real estate, it's Location, Location, Location. In marketing, it's Repeat, Repeat, Repeat.

Brands aren't born in a day. If you want to create awareness, enthusiasm, and buy-in of your internal brand, keep repeating the messages until they become second nature. And keep them consistent.

If you repeat the same messages over and over, you'll start creating an A+ brand. That's what Richard Berman did to turn a school from a bankrupt lost cause into a thriving community. Berman took over the presidency of Manhattanville College in Westchester, New York, about 18 months before the date bond insurers threatened to shut it down. Berman breathed new life into the school by creating a distinct—and ubiquitous—internal brand.

He started by developing the mission of the college and a set of values that was compelling for all stakeholders, and then repeating those values as many times and in as many ways as he could. He incorporated them into every speech, brochure, and decision he made at the college. They were built into the curriculum (the product); the extracurricular activities, the computer labs, and the dorm life (customer service); and the orientation of new faculty and staff (internal).

"I was essentially doing brand management," Berman said.

Berman's internal and external branding paid off. The school now had focus and clarity like it never had before, and Berman's administration was able to build momentum around their brand; rally students, teachers and administrators, and the community; and bring the college back to life. Manhattanville College is now a thriving community of more than 1,500 undergraduate students and 1,000 graduate students, and it continues to grow. In the past nine years since Berman implemented his Four Values, the college has more than tripled its endowment and net assets, and has been profitable every year for the past eight years. *U.S. News & World Report* ranks it in the top tier in its category, and the college attracts high quality students from all over the world. Berman directly attributes the college's success to his administration's internal and external marketing and branding efforts, saying, "It's the reason we turned this place around."

Remember that creating a brand takes time. Berman's success was the result of years of persistent, consistent branding. Fortunately, there are usually some signs of progress even in the early stages of branding, but it does require patience! As Berman can attest, it really does pay off.

What Should Your Brand Look Like?

An internal branding campaign should have a logo, just as your external brand does. If you decide to use the same brand then there's no need to design a new logo. But if you want to communicate a unique set of messages to your internal audiences, then you may decide to go with a new and distinct logo. If that is the case, rule number one is hire a professional designer who understands branding. The designer should show you some ideas that complement your external logo. It may take visual cues from the external logo, including some of the same shapes, fonts, colors, and/or motifs. The idea is to build on the same emotional connection your external brand evokes.

In addition to the logo, you'll need to use other related graphics for branding. You can use colors and shapes from the logo in unusual places to subtly keep the brand present at all times without actually using the logo itself. Disney uses this technique—a "wink"—very effectively. You've no doubt seen the silhouette of Mickey Mouse's head and ears. It's classic Disney. You'd know that shape anywhere even though it's not literally the Disney logo itself. At Disney World, you'll see the shape in landscaping features, carpet patterns, bathroom fixtures, and who knows how many thousands of other places. When you visit, see how many you can find. What a fun treasure hunt! And what a great way this is for Disney to deliver a happy, positive image of its brand.

According to Glyn Lobo, partner at the international law firm Dechert LLP, even upscale law firms are embracing traditional branding concepts. His firm has devoted considerable resources to a consistent brand image both internally and externally by using the company logo, colors, and other branding elements on all of its internal and external documents and deliverables. It has recently required a consistent format for its e-mail signatures as well. Consistency ensures that a company's brand will be continually reinforced inside and out to maximize its impact.

Branding an internal initiative follows the same principles as creating an internal brand for the company, with just a few twists.

How to Create a Powerful Internal Marketing Campaign for Your Initiative

The branding for an initiative should always be closely tied to, but distinct from, the company's brand. Unlike day-to-day internal branding, the branding of an internal initiative has a short shelf life. Remember that a streamlined approach is best—too much message clutter diminishes the power of your internal marketing campaign. Choose one or two themes that are consistent with and complementary to the rest of your branding. Make It Hampton is a perfect example of unique internal branding that reinforces the external brand of the company.

Take branding cues from your company's advertising and marketing campaigns. For instance, FedEx used its popular advertising slogan, "absolutely, positively" in its internal marketing campaign to address the pilots' strike. It was also used in their external branding campaigns.

Brand messaging for change initiatives and crisis control should create a sense of urgency in your audience to facilitate immediate action. The most effective brands and slogans are action-oriented. This type of brand or slogan can help create motivation and momentum. It can also lend itself to several different media as a rallying cry—a call to action—and it's more likely to make it into the common lexicon of the company.

BRAND FANATICS

Now that you've defined your internal brand, the internal marketing campaign begins in earnest. Just like in classical marketing cycles, the goal is to communicate your brand as much, as often, and in as many ways as possible so that your employees will become fanatics about delivering your brand promise.

Want to know how the top brands in the world do it? If you don't have a seven-figure budget to pay for consultants and branding gurus, take a look at these internal branding campaigns of some of the top brands and maybe it will give you some good ideas.

Coca-Cola. King of all brands, Coke wanted to establish itself as a company that cares about more than just profits. It launched an internal and external marketing campaign that branded "Close to Home." The campaign targeted specific audiences by using the subbrands, Close to Our People, Close to Our Partners, and Close to Our Communities. The brand names work because they evoke a friendly, cozy feeling that warms up its cool, refreshing brand image. (A blast from the past: In 1971, Coke introduced a TV commercial featuring people from around the world standing on a hillside singing, "I'd like to buy the world a Coke." The song was so popular it was eventually recorded as a single under the title, "I'd Like to Teach the World to Sing." For the full story, go to http://www.cocacola.com and select "heritage" and then "Coke-lore." It's worth the visit.)

Sony. Right up there among the world's greatest brands, Sony is one of the few companies that can get away with launching a branding campaign that is simply, confidently called "Being Sony." According to Sony's press statements, the campaign is an "extensive, companywide initiative in the U.S. designed to foster a common understanding of the Sony brand among employees, customers, and consumers."

McDonald's. The company launched a universal marketing program both externally and internally using the advertising slogan "I'm Loving It." The idea, according to a McDonald's press release, is to "provide consistency in messaging and communications to customers and employees." It's hard to get much more direct or emphatic than this message.

Nike. Nike uses one of the oldest forms of communication to keep its rich heritage alive from one generation to the next—storytelling. One of the first things new employees learn when they walk through the doors is the company's folklore, an important part of what has made Nike what it is today. They hear stories about the founding of the company and the heroics not of the athletic stars in their commercials, but of the stars within the company. Here's one we like: Coach Bowerman thought his team needed better running shoes, so he went out to his workshop and poured rubber into the family waffle iron, thus creating the innovative waffle-textured sole!

Microsoft. Microsoft took advantage of its reputation for having some of the smartest minds within its walls. It named its internal branding campaign "Realizing Potential," with the tagline: Your potential. Our passion. The campaign features images of people achieving their dreams—thanks to Microsoft's imaginative software.

Some very smart people conjured up these campaign slogans. Smart people just like the people with whom you work. Give them a chance. Let your team get involved. They might just create an internal brand that fits your company like a glove. And what could be a more effective brand than one that employees help to build and define, and that honestly expresses how they feel about it. That's what we call a "beautiful" brand.

QUIZ
Are You "Selling" Your Company To Your Employees?

What's that? You already do internal marketing? Great! Then take this quiz and see how you and your company score when it comes to internal branding.

If you're a top executive of your company, you should (hopefully) be able to answer these questions easily yourself, but try giving it to your employees and see how they do. If you're an employee, take this test yourself first, and then ask other employees in your company to take it. If you're a consultant working with companies who may need to improve internal marketing, give this quiz to your clients and see how they do. It could be an eye-opener for a lot of companies. You may need an internal branding campaign more than you know. Be sure to give this test to behind-the-scenes employees in IT, finance, and HR, as well as those employees who are closer to the customer and may know the company's products and services better. Good internal marketing should touch everyone in an organization.

HOW WELL DO YOU KNOW YOUR COMPANY?

1. In what year was your company founded?
   _____

2. What are your company's vision, mission, and/or values?
   _____
   _____
   _____

3. Name three branding devices that your company uses (logo, slogans, taglines, etc.)?
   _____
   _____
   _____

4. Who are your top three competitors?

　　_____
　　_____
　　_____

5. What are your company's main strategic goals for this year?

　　_____
　　_____
　　_____

6. Name some of the trends/changes that your industry is expected to go through in the coming year.

　　_____
　　_____
　　_____

HOW WELL DO YOU KNOW YOUR PRODUCTS AND/OR SERVICES?

7. What are your company's best-selling products or services?

　　_____
　　_____　_____
　　_____

8. Have you used your company's products/services (if applicable)?

　　_____
　　_____
　　_____

HOW WELL DO YOU KNOW YOUR JOB?

9. When was the last time you received any job training?

　　_____

10. When was the last time you received performance feedback from your manager?

   _____

11. When was the last time you sat down with your manager to talk about your career goals?

   _____

HOW WELL DO YOU KNOW THE LATEST NEWS?

12. When was the last time your company shared news of its latest developments with you?

   _____

13. When was the last time you received any communication from your company's leader?

   _____

ANSWER KEY

Give yourself the following points for each question.

Questions 1-8: 1 point for each correctly answered question. (For question 8, if you said "yes," score 1 point.)

Question 9: 2 points if you received training within the last three months; **1 point** if you received training within the last six months. **Deduct a point** if you haven't received any training within the last 12 months.

Question 10: 2 points if you received feedback from your manager (or another supervisor, but not a peer) within the last month; **1 point** if you received feedback within the last six months. **Deduct a point** if you haven't received any feedback in the last 12 months.

Question 11: 2 points if your supervisor sat down with you within the last three months to talk about your career goals and expectations; **1 point** if it happened within the last six months. **Deduct a point** if you haven't had that conversation in the last 12 months. **Subtract 2 points** if you're not sure who your manager is or if you've never heard of performance management.

Question 12: 2 points if your company has given you an update within the last week; **1 point** if it has been a month. **Deduct a point** if it seems like nothing new has happened in your company in *forever*. If something big happened at your company and you had to find out from a newspaper, morning news program, or your peers around the water cooler, **deduct 2 points.**

Question 13: 2 points if your company's headquarters/leadership communicated with you in some way today; **1 point** if it's been less than a week. If it's been more than a month without word from your fearless leaders, **deduct a point.** If the last communication you received didn't make any sense or you didn't believe a word of what was being communicated, **subtract 2 points.** If you don't know who your leadership is, you're not sure if they're even alive, and you really couldn't care less, **subtract 4 points.**

If you scored **15 to 21 points,** congratulations! Your company is doing a great job with internal marketing, and you probably could have helped us write this book!

If you scored **10 to 15 points,** not bad. You probably have an internal marketing plan in place and you're trying your best. Brush up on your skills by taking a few tips from this book.

If you scored **1 to 10 points,** keep reading! You obviously need it.

If you scored **–10 to 0 points,** seek professional help! Read this book at least five times and call us in the morning.

Chapter

4

DOING YOUR HOMEWORK

Absolutely everyone contributes in some way to dreaming up, manufacturing, or delivering your product or service. You surely want them all working toward a goal of excellence.

"If people from the top to the bottom of your organization don't understand your strategy, then you don't have one," says Dr. Daniel Denison, professor of management and organization at the International Institute for Management Development (IMD) in Lausanne, Switzerland. "You may have a mission, a vision, or a business plan, but without alignment and understanding across levels, no one can implement a business strategy."

There are eight steps to implementing a successful internal marketing program.

1. Set a course from A to B.
2. Define your audiences.
3. Assess the climate.
4. Define your key messages.

5. Match vehicles to the message.
6. Choose your champions.
7. Now, execute the plan.
8. Measure and adapt.

In the next three chapters we'll cover each of these topics so that you have a road map for implementation.

DIGGING FOR TREASURE

Doing the research for your internal marketing plan is like digging for treasure—the more you unearth, the richer you get. While you may be anxious to get to the action part of your plan, be patient. Otherwise, you could end up with results like Christopher Columbus. When he left he didn't know where he was going. When he got there, he didn't know where he was. When he returned, he didn't know where he'd been. You certainly don't want to emulate his results. (Then again, despite his confusion, he still gets a lot of accolades.)

Of the entire eight-step internal marketing process, more than one-third is devoted to doing your homework. This chapter tells you how.

STEP 1: SET A COURSE FROM A TO B

Analyze the Situation

Step back and take a look at the situation at hand. What do you hope to accomplish? What problem are you trying to solve, or what improvement are you trying to incorporate? Ask yourself, "Are the current circumstances in my organization conducive to achieving our goals?" Is your company healthy or struggling? How does your company fare against competitors? Is the employee climate supportive or adversary? What is your company's reputation as an employer? Have you recently experienced any serious setbacks?

What do your employees feel about past and current initiatives? Have similar efforts been successful in the past or have they been seen as another "flavor of the month" project? Have you involved employees before, or is this a new approach?

Marketing firms use something called a SWOT analysis to help them design external marketing plans. A SWOT analysis evaluates your strengths, weaknesses, opportunities, and threats. While they use this technique for external purposes, you'll do it from an internal perspective.

Strengths

Ask yourself: What are our organization's strengths and how can we leverage them to make this a success? What did we do right in our last successful initiative?

When you are assessing your strengths, try to view things through the eyes of your employees. Spend some time asking people at all levels what they think your strengths are. They undoubtedly have a different perspective than you do, so you'll get a clearer view of reality this way. We've seen many examples of management being surprised by unexpectedly low employee opinion survey scores, only to realize that there's a gap between their perception and reality. Taking a little time with them really helps to start the initiative off on the right foot. It shows your employees that you aren't merely "pushing" something on them but asking them to be involved. This helps to build buy-in and ownership immediately. Some strengths you may discover are creativity, flexibility, talented people, technology, curiosity, and openness.

Weaknesses

What lessons did you learn from past failed initiatives? What is it that you do not want to repeat? Did employees blast you for that last "big initiative" because there wasn't enough leadership direction, communication, or "insert gripe here"? Talk to employees about what they think are your company's weaknesses. As they tell you their opinions, ask them to share their ideas on how these can be resolved. Most companies don't ask employees to help determine how to fix what's broken. You'll be amazed at the ideas you discover.

When consulting, we always ask clients before beginning a project, "On a scale of 1 to 10, we want your satisfaction with us to be a perfect score. What would it take for us to get this 10?" Ask your employees what it would take to get a perfect score from them.

Employee meetings can unearth some amazing information. We began a study with a health care client by asking employees what they felt management could do to earn a 10. We expected them to talk about things like overtime pay, time off, and other personal issues. They didn't. They asked for items that would help them better care for patients, and they asked for better communication. What a wonderful thing for management to see. Employees were not the whiny, nothing-satisfies-them people the bosses initially thought. It was much easier for management to feel good about the process knowing that employees most wanted what was best for the patients and the organization.

In another situation, we were conducting employee focus groups for a client's change initiative and discovered something awful. Many of their managers said they didn't believe that the executives had been authentic or truthful in their communications in previous initiatives. Imagine the kind of climate that created.

We were not going to fall into that trap. Our first order of business was to make honest communication a priority. As a matter of fact, we helped management be so forthcoming, employees must have thought we dumped a truckload of truth serum in the executives' coffee. The execs held candid conference calls with every single employee in attendance. We offered nearly 3,000 employees the chance to hear it straight from the horse's mouth. Ever hear of open-book management? Well, this book's spine was cracked wide open.

When planning your internal marketing initiative, you may be able to determine some of your weaknesses from human resource statistics like turnover rates, or from employee satisfaction surveys. But nothing beats sitting face to face with employees to dig deeper into their perceptions.

Without focus groups, interviews, and other types of information gathering, we never would learn the very specific information we need to make initiatives a huge success!

Opportunities

This part should be fun! Give yourself a chance to dream big. If this internal marketing initiative is successful, it could affect attitudes and results throughout your organization. Think about what you could gain, such as:

- Motivated employees who are more apt to take on additional responsibilities because they feel they've been rewarded for their hard work
- Lower employee turnover, saving thousands of dollars in hiring and training
- Happy employees, which leads to happier customers, which ultimately translates to long-term loyalty and new customers through word of mouth
- Increased trust and support for future changes
- Greater likelihood of budget allocation for future initiatives

When you begin to dream, don't put limits on your ideas or counter every suggestion with a "yeah, but . . . " statement. Until you begin to practice internal marketing you can't begin to understand the depth of change it enables. You will be able to experience changes that range from small potatoes to caviar.

Threats

Internal threats create external threats, right? In fact, internal threats can directly translate to driving customers away. Some examples of internal threats that can impact your business and your customer loyalty are:

- Poor company culture that breeds politics
- Unhappy, disgruntled employees who badmouth the company and share their apathy, irritation, or unhappiness with anyone who will listen (including customers)
- Employees who feel no ownership or loyalty, leading to lackadaisical performance, an overall attitude of just "putting in their time," or high turnover
- Lack of employee training, which can cause your business to fall behind in product development, sales, service, and efficiency
- Insufficient tools to do the work
- Outdated technology
- "Baggage" from previous management mistakes
- Interdepartmental strife

Internal marketing can't fix all of these issues, but it can definitely alleviate people's negative feelings about them.

Ask yourself these questions: How does corporate culture filter down to customers? Is it friendly and attentive, or is it negative in ways that could make customers uncomfortable?

This book would not be complete without a classic airline story. We've shared several positive stories about Southwest Airlines' superb service. Now here's a story from the alternative point of view.

As a super-quadruple-diamond-platinum-gold flier I am fortunate to have earned some benefits, one being an almost guaranteed upgrade to first class. I booked a flight to San Antonio, but somehow the computer system didn't enter my frequent flier number. My associate, Tim, was joining me from a connecting flight, and I had hoped to upgrade him as well (another miles-related perk). I went to the gate agent to inquire.

"Hi, I'm a platinum member, and I'm on the wait list for an upgrade," I said. "I was hoping you could check on that for me, and also see if I could upgrade my travel partner. He's coming in . . . "

"I don't even know who you are," she interrupted. "I can't do anything without knowing who you are."

She certainly put me in my place. What could I have been thinking? What an idiot I am. Perhaps I don't even deserve to fly. I was in the wrong.

It's a lot to convey in two short sentences, but she was a pro. I now understood my intellectual limitations.

I try to live by a theory I call BOD—benefit of the doubt. When I encounter people who act as this woman did, I imagine that they might have a personal problem that is weighing heavy on their minds. Maybe her dog just ran away or a loved one is seriously ill, both good reasons for acting out of sorts. In this case, I sat down and took a few minutes to try to change my attitude because, truth is, when it first happened I wanted to punch her out.

After a while my travel partner arrived, and he had already been upgraded. Luckily, we didn't have to go back to the gate agent to ask. With just minutes before boarding time, Tim and I walked up to the boarding area. A redcap was just bringing a wheelchair off the plane, having assisted a customer in advance of full boarding.

Standing next to us was an extremely elderly lady, bent over, using a cane to steady herself. Her daughter held her arm as they stepped toward the agent. As the wheelchair passed, they moved toward the door and handed the agent their boarding passes, expecting to get on the plane early, just like the other passenger who needed assistance. How dare they? Ms. Pit Bull looked at them with disgust. "I haven't even called for boarding," she snarled. "It would be better for me if you wait."

Better for me? Did she really say that? Tim's eyebrows and mine rose a full two inches.

The lady and her daughter dutifully stepped back from the door and waited.

After we boarded, Tim asked me if I had some ibuprofen. I said no, but that I had aspirin. I handed him the bottle. He looked at me and said, "You know, it would be better for me if you carried ibuprofen." We had a hearty laugh over that one. "Better for me" became the theme of that trip.

One of three things was happening here:

1. Something serious actually was going on in the gate agent's life. If that was the case, we apologize for using her as an example of poor service.
2. The agent is an honest-to-goodness jerk and no amount of marketing, training, or other type of program is going to turn her into a charmer.
3. The woman had no idea that she was doing something wrong because she hadn't been instructed how to deal with customers. Or maybe she had no commitment to being a stellar representative of her company's goals. She may not even realize her company is in the *service* industry.

In the first two cases, internal marketing won't help. But in the third instance—ignorance of the need or the way to serve—a good dose of internal marketing could improve her customers' experience, and could make her day brighter, too.

If your culture tolerates an "it's better for me" attitude, it will logically lead to a serious external threat.

Taking care of internal threats seriously decreases the risk of external threats. That's the name of the game.

GOAL FOR IT! SETTING YOUR GOALS AND OBJECTIVES

When authors Tom Peters and Nancy Austin wrote *A Passion for Excellence,* they cited a statement from an executive of a high-tech company. He said, "The most important marketer in our company is the man or woman on the loading dock who decides not to drop the damned box into the back of a truck."

To us, that statement represents the ultimate in service strategies. Great customer experiences are created on an unbroken string of great employee performances. Reminders all along the string ensure that employees know their roles in achieving the company's goals.

But wait. Time out. Think about that phrase, *the company's goals.* I'm reminded of how goals work in a marriage. Suppose the garbage is piling up in the kitchen. One spouse says to the other, "Honey, would you take the garbage out?" The other spouse says, "Sure, I'll be happy to help you." There is an implicit message here that the "helper" spouse is just assisting the other in carrying out his or her goals. How much better would it be if both spouses shared the goal of keeping a clean house? Both would be motivated to take out the garbage because they each have a personal investment in a clean house. No longer would one spouse have to ask the other to help.

In reality, we want employees to own the goals. If employees have a personal investment in the goals, they're more motivated than if they're helping the company carry out its goals. It takes a lot of tools to create outstanding performance—training, feedback, rewards, recognition, and so on. But all of these tools should begin with an understanding of why each employee came to work for the company, and that is to deliver the brand promise and satisfy customers. That is the *shared* goal.

Creating Goals

Begin with the end in mind. When the initiative is implemented, what do you want to happen? What do your employees want to happen? Make your goals measurable and realistic, such as "reduce employee turnover by 10 percent" rather than "eliminate turnover."

When we say measurable and realistic, we mean not too lofty or too far in the future. People have short attention spans, and they need to know they can reach a milestone.

Keep goals to a small number, say three or so. Make sure you have a laser focus on what you really want to accomplish for the initiative and make it tangible. For example, in one internal marketing campaign we did, we started with a goal of creating awareness within each of our audiences for a major initiative. It was a small, attainable goal, and it was good enough to get us started.

The rubber hits the road when you get to objectives and measurement. Your goals are just goals until you actually attach some action steps to them.

Creating Objectives

Next up, objectives. Objectives are the actionable part or the actual steps you will take to help you to reach your initiative's goals. Here's an example of an objective that will guide efforts: By the completion of phase one of the XYZ initiative, the project team will have developed a ten-minute presentation to explain the key goals of the initiative to other employees.

Notice that the objective is simple (develop a ten-minute presentation), the deadline is defined (by the end of phase one), and it can be measured (Did they do it or not?). Finally, you can determine the effectiveness of the presentation by surveying employees to see if they understand the message.

There's a good test called SMART that works well for writing objectives. It serves as a guide to create and set realistic yet measurable objectives. Ask yourself these five questions to determine if your objectives are SMART:

1. Specific: Does my objective clearly specify what I want to achieve?
2. Measurable: Will I be able to measure whether I am meeting the objectives or not?
3. Achievable: Are my objectives achievable and attainable?
4. Realistic: Can I realistically achieve the objectives with the resources I have?
5. Time-bound: By when do I want or need to achieve the set objectives?

Let's try out this formula. Here's the same objective expressed in a different way: By the completion of phase one of the XYZ initiative, the project team will be able to identify the key goals of the initiative and be able to appropriately explain the initiative's mission to others with 80 percent satisfaction.

Notice the example above specifies what we are looking to achieve with the project team for this particular goal (the project team will be able to identify the key goals and be able to explain the initiative to others). It's also measurable. We're going to strive for 80 percent satisfaction. We can measure satisfaction by using a quantitative Web survey striving to get four out of our five points to reach the 80 percent level. It's also achievable because it is something that can be done. We're not launching an employee into space after all. And it's realistic. We want to look at what we can realistically get done and that fills the bill within the amount of time we are allotting (by the end of phase one of our initiative). One last piece of advice: Make sure you have objectives for each of your goals and keep them manageable at about four or five objectives per goal.

STEP 2: KNOW YOUR AUDIENCES

Marketing to internal audiences is more complicated than you might think. In fact, few corporate plans take into account the diversity of audiences. Usually the plan includes a newsletter, a magazine, an all-employee meeting, occasional e-mails and one employee awards dinner. That's an oversimplification, of course, but not by much. The sheer fact is that an internal marketing program is not as simple as figuring out what vehicles you can use based on the amount of money you have to spend.

So how *should* it be done?

First, think about to whom you want to market. Start with the macro view. Consider everyone who can help or hinder your efforts. Here are a few to consider:

- Customer-facing employees
- Managers
- Support teams (administrative assistants, clerks, etc.)
- Other department teams
- Senior management group
- Board of directors
- Customer service

And don't forget the dockworker who puts the box on the truck. There are hundreds of nooks and crannies in your company that can easily be overlooked. Your message must penetrate them all. In the Make It Hampton project we mentioned in Chapter 3, we had 15 important audiences. It wasn't easy to reach them all consistently, but it was a vital component to the project's success.

Next, before you communicate, you should learn as much about your audience as possible. In an ideal world, you would go to their location and spend time working alongside them. In the normal world, you can find out a lot by talking with a handful of people from each position type.

Consider each audience's characteristics, keeping in mind:

- Education level and whether they speak English as a second language (especially if you are communicating with employees outside the United States).
- Demographics, including their location, age, gender, income levels, type of position, and so on.

Maslow's Hierarchy of Needs

In the mid-1940s through the 1950s, Abraham Maslow developed a theory that human beings have inherent needs that are divided into five levels: physiological, safety, belonging and love, esteem, and self-actualization. Each level must be satisfied before a person addresses the next. For example, his theory proposes that people don't worry much about their esteem unless their basic needs like food and shelter are satisfied. So, even though we live in a society where individuals search for self-actualization, they still need food and shelter before they go to yoga class.

Every audience has unique needs, both as a group and as individuals within the group.

For example, a single mother trying to support three kids on a line-level worker's salary may not be especially motivated by receiving a PDA as a reward for outstanding performance.

Not that we're trying to turn you into humanists or suggest that you explore all the ins and outs of psychology. We merely ask that you take Maslow's theory to its simplest form: What's in it for me? When you can identify how your initiative can benefit each of your audiences, you'll have a good idea of how to position information to reach them.

Vary Your Audience by Message and Vary Your Message by Audience

So how can Maslow's needs theory translate into creating an effective message? Here are two things to consider:

1. How will your audience vary by message?
2. How will your message vary by audience?

Let's look at each of those. The simpler of the two is determining how your audience will vary by message. Are there some things that certain groups just don't need or want to know? Don't answer too quickly. We've heard executives say that line-level employees don't need to know about things like the company's recapitalization. But when we worked with a manufacturing plant we learned that the factory workers were more informed than we were about the financial health of the organization, they were dedicated to following the stock price, and they were always keen to see the annual report. Before you rule out an audience, give it some thought.

Internally, the audience will often vary by message. For example, assume you are the CEO and you're talking about upcoming department budgets. Your audience would most likely be your small group of direct reports who are responsible for compiling the information. You wouldn't need to report this process to the broad employee population. (But to be safe, you might want to alert employees that budget time is approaching so they'll know why their boss is so testy!)

On the other hand, if you're announcing a merger, you would clearly need to speak to your entire employee population. Even those employees whose jobs won't be affected will be anxious, curious, and no doubt unsettled by the news.

Now, how about varying your message by audience? Let's see how this works. You are an executive with a major restaurant chain that is almost exclusively franchised. There's a big change in menu items on the boards for next year. It will require an investment by owners and a change in procedures by the general managers.

First, we know that you have two audiences:

1. Franchise restaurant owners
2. Store general managers

How would you handle each one?

1. To owners, your message would be fairly strategic, describing the reason for the change, how it enhances your competitive edge, how much it will cost, and how you expect it will improve margins.
2. To store managers, the message would be more tactical. They need to know about food ordering, training employees, replacing menus, and so on.

In both cases, you need to describe a change in menus, but you share different levels of information based on what is most important to each. This is just one example of varying a message by audience. This type of targeting is called *positioning*.

Positioning Is Not Little White Lies

Positioning is a way of directing a message to the needs of a particular group. It helps people understand what is happening and why, and how it will affect the company or its employees.

Let's get this out of the way right now: Positioning information is not spin-doctoring, nor is it lying or doctoring the truth. Positioning is about helping others understand a message in a way that applies to them.

Here's an example of how a message looks different when it's reported versus positioned.

First, the reported version: Hampton Inn will be requiring its hotel franchise owners to make 4.2 million changes in its hotels over a nine-month period. From now on, the quality auditors will be checking to make sure every hotel abides by the new standards.

All of that was true. But now let's look at the positioned version: Hampton Inn and a number of its franchise owners and general managers have worked together to identify ways the hotels can enhance their guests' experiences in both tangible and intangible ways. The changes are based on guest feedback and competitive data. The corporation has invested almost $10 million in research and testing. It will also help offset the owners' required investment by paying for installation of the breakfast component in every hotel.

This statement is also true. Notice how the first version that states "just the facts" doesn't tell you anything about why the changes are coming. It looks like a mandate coming from on high, not to be questioned or ignored. If you were an owner, how would you feel about reading that statement? Not exactly warm and fluffy, I'll bet.

And how do you suppose general managers would react to such an announcement? While the owners might be signing the checks, the general managers bear the burden of making the changes in the hotels and training their staffs in the new procedures. They will probably be left with a lot of questions, uncertainty, and, potentially, resentment.

The positioned statement, on the other hand, explains the changes in a way that is likely to make them more acceptable to both owners and general managers. It shows that the decisions were collaborative, that owners' concerns and needs were heard and taken into account, and that the changes represent things the guests want. Best of all, it tells people that the corporation has and will invest its own dollars.

That is positioning.

TARGET PRACTICE

Think about how advertisers target their advertising. They examine who buys their products and design ads to appeal to their most important customer groups. They call these *market segments.* A segment might be defined as young families, affluent seniors, Hispanic professionals ages 25–35, or urban African Americans. You will segment your internal groups that the same way, defining your internal "customers" and determining which groups will "buy" your message.

Suppose you are head of a hospital. You will have audiences such as the professional staff of nurses and medical teams, the doctors group, the administrative staff, the custodial staff, and perhaps the dietary workers.

In each case, you will consider the needs of the group. We're not experts in health care, but we can imagine what's on the minds of certain groups. The nurses are thinking of patient care, adequate staffing, available time off, and pay levels. The physicians may be concerned with patient care, scheduling of surgical facilities, and having the equipment they need. Your administrative team could be challenged by short staffing and recruiting problems, as well as parking and development opportunities.

Direct Effect

Each of your audiences is concerned about priorities that may or may not affect other groups. Thus, your communication will be most effective if you direct it to each group's individual concerns. This means that it may not be wise to use one overarching communication such as a newsletter or a meeting. Depending on the message, you may need to tailor several different media to address the concerns of each group, alternating vehicles that reinforce your message. Perhaps you begin with a series of meetings, send an e-mail, and follow up with a print document that recaps the issues and answers.

The Poor Second or Third Shift

Few employees are as isolated as those who work the night shift. Factory workers, health care providers, 24-hour help-line operators, security guards, convenience store employees—all of these suffer from a gargantuan communications gap. They're not around when management holds meetings. They're not around when celebrations are held. They're not around when major announcements are made. In short, they are the victims of the dreaded night shift blues, a malady that leads to a feeling of abandonment and alienation. Their allegiance is mostly to their shift team because these are the people who help them make it through the night.

In some cases, we find that the night shift team is more like a group of workers from a different company than they are coworkers of the employees who work in the daytime.

How do you overcome the barriers? It's inevitable. Be there when they are. There is no better way to demonstrate you care about their needs than to stay up all night and see what goes on. You may find out that the area in which they work isn't lighted well enough for them to read. Or that they're part of a skeleton crew without time to learn about company information. Perhaps they don't have access to the VHS player in the training room to watch videotaped corporate messages.

The possibilities for failing to meet their needs are high unless you make a concerted effort to reach them where they are.

Off-site Workers

How many times have you heard someone complain that the home office doesn't understand the needs of the off-site locations? Well, that's because they don't. I find that often (very often) when the people at headquarters want to communicate with line-level employees, they forget the great divide that separates them.

Consider this: The line-level employee relates to his or her supervisor. The supervisor relates to the manager of the off-site office. The manager may report to a regional director, or may answer to someone at headquarters. Count the number of levels between home office management and line-level employees. It's probably between three and five. Chances are that the line-level employees don't associate their jobs with anything beyond the location where they work, much less all the way to headquarters. It's pretty tough to deliver information to those team members when they may not know who you are or care, or even have a clue why you're talking to them!

We say this to illustrate that messages that skip multiple levels have a better chance of being received when they're delivered by the person or group to which employees most closely relate. In a case where your audience is widespread and multileveled, you may want to call upon a local supervisor or someone who has direct influence to serve as the messenger. The supervisor is, after all, the most influential person in the audience's work life.

People Who Work for You but Don't Work for You

Some organizations have important internal audiences that do not work for them directly. This makes internal marketing a huge challenge for two reasons:

1. You do not directly control their paychecks, so they don't have accountability to you for their performance. You can't tell them what to do.
2. You must maintain an amiable relationship with their true bosses, so you can't be particularly direct or blunt in asking employees to buy your message. The actual boss wants to maintain control over what his or her employees place as a priority.

This triangular situation requires a lot of the secret ingredient—persuasion. To get people on board you must inspire them to want to get on board.

Take for example a situation in a company that is heavily franchised. Pretend you are the senior vice president of Hampton Inn, and you want to send a message to all of the line-level employees at the Hampton Inn hotels across the country. Now hold that thought.

The vast majority of Hampton Inn hotels are owned by others, meaning that a small minority of employees actually work for Hampton Inn. In some cases, the hotels are a part of a hotel management company, so Hampton Inn's primary relationship is with the management company, and the relationship with the hotel employees is even farther removed.

Now, try to follow this path: In a franchised situation, hotel line-level employees' loyalty is first to their supervisor, then to their general manager and hotel, then to their owners or management companies, and finally, in a precarious and mostly invisible way, to the hotel's brand. Ask a room attendant in Concord, New Hampshire, what she thinks of working for Hilton Hotels Corporation and she will probably look at you as if you have two heads. Yes, in a perfect world, she would know that the Hampton Inn brand is a part of Hilton Hotels Corporation. But that's a stretch from reality.

If the senior vice president of the Hampton Inn brand sent a letter to the maintenance engineer in Tupelo, Mississippi, the maintenance engineer might very well say, "Who the hell is Phil Cordell? And what does this have to do with my preventive maintenance plan?"

There are unique challenges associated with internal marketing to such a broad and far-flung audience, many of whom don't know why you're talking to them and have no interest in what you have to say.

Contract Workers

Another situation in which you have nonemployees is when outside contractors work on or off your premises. Many companies have technical groups such as IT consultants who are assigned to long-term projects and work on-site. Although they are not officially employees, they are a vital part of your team. It's true that you can ignore them and still get the job done. But how much more motivated and loyal would they feel if you include them in your "family"? Great attitudes are contagious, and run on a two-way street. Because their attitude can certainly affect your employees, it pays to keep them in the loop.

STEP 3: ASSESS THE CLIMATE

What is the climate in your organization? No, really, what is the climate? What are your employees thinking? Are they happy? Disgruntled? Trusting or suspicious? Do they have fun in their jobs, or do they consider their work drudgery? Are they being affected by tough economic times, or enjoying a healthy economy? Do they support senior management, or are they defensive and argumentative? All of these questions will help you determine what the climate is in your company, and how receptive or resistant people will be to your message.

Most CEOs have a rosier view of their company than what is reality. Few care to admit that their employees are miserably unhappy, unmotivated, surly, uncooperative, disloyal, or back-biting. After all, these negative feelings can reflect on their ability to lead. Most will say climate of their company is about as good as, or somewhat better than, that of other organizations. Most also feel that their areas of concern are merely opportunities for improvement. In reality, the situation is usually far worse than they realize.

The starting point for figuring out how to build an internal marketing plan is by conducting a rigorously honest assessment of the situation. (And remember, if your company's performance isn't what you hope for, it's pretty likely that the climate is not 100 percent healthy.)

The best way to assess the climate is to ask the employees. What a concept! In our careers, we have done many, many interviews in companies, first asking management for their opinions of the situation, and then asking employees. Most of the time, management says: "We don't really need a survey. We're attuned to our employees. We know what they think and feel." We rarely have seen a company in which management had a clear picture of employees' feelings. Even if you think you know what employees are feeling, it's better to ask, just to be safe.

Here are some other questions that you can ask yourself while you're waiting for the employee climate survey results: What's been happening in the company lately? Have there been any major changes such as a merger or acquisition? Have there been any layoffs or reorganizations? Is there a new high-level executive? Is the CEO respected? Loved? Feared? Hated? Ignored?

How is the company's financial health? Are performance results up or down from the previous year? Is the stock price stable or rising? Has the company recently experienced a steep decline in the stock price? How is the economy affecting the company's financial health, positively or negatively?

Are the company's customer satisfaction scores high or low? Is business seasonal? Are there high stress times with regular let-ups, or is the company a constant pressure cooker? Do most employees have a balanced work/personal life, or are they stressed-out workaholics?

Is the company's pay scale on a par with the industry and the community? Is the employee population generally satisfied or unsatisfied? Are the company's health care benefits good? Does the company have to deal with a workers union?

All of these questions will help you define whether employees will be receptive to your efforts to deliver your brand message or whether they will reject it. If you decide your climate is healthy, you may assume that your employees will be happy to hear what you have to say. But wait. Remember the great and powerful law of change: 99 percent of the population resists change and feels anxious about it, whether the change is good or bad. If what you have to say involves changing the way people perceive or work for your company, you have a little more work to do.

THE FUN BEGINS

Now that you've done your homework, you're ready to put all your knowledge to work to create your plan. But the treasure hunt should not stop here; keep collecting information so that you can reflect and adapt as you go. Internal marketing is a dynamic process, and one you can continuously expand and improve.

Ready to go? Turn to Chapter 5 to begin your plan.

Chapter 5

WHAT TO SAY TO WHOM AND HOW

You've looked around and looked within your organization, so you should have a pretty clear picture of your communication environment. This is where some companies douse the flame by jumping ahead and implementing programs. Our advice is to once again take your time. In this chapter, we discuss how to evaluate what messages you should be sending, to which audiences, and through what media.

Two-way communication is really a three-element process. For communication to be two-way, the message must be sent, received, and understood. This means that you may have to change the words you use, vary the vehicle or vehicles you employ, and even vary the spokesperson who delivers the message. Just because you send information out doesn't mean people "get it" or can act on it. It's much more complicated than writing an e-mail or giving a speech.

In this chapter, we'll show you how to match your message and your vehicles to your audiences. And how to make sure that the message you sent is the message they heard.

STEP 4: DEFINE YOUR KEY MESSAGES

Several years ago, Hilton Hotels Corporation acquired Promus Hotels, which owned the Hampton Inn, Homewood Suites, Embassy Suites, Doubletree, and Red Lion hotel brands. News of the acquisition was somewhat warmly received by corporate management on both sides, who saw the deal as one that would leverage the combined power of all the brands plus the Hilton name. There were financial implications, naturally, and, for one of the groups, there was the potential for a corporate move to Hilton's Beverly Hills headquarters. For that one group, anxiety ran high about whether they'd soon become the Beverly Hillbillies.

While corporate employees waited anxiously for word of how their stock options might be affected and whether their benefits would change, room attendants at the hotels just wondered whether they could get ten cents an hour more if they moved to the hotel down the street.

If you believe in Maslow's hierarchy of needs, it's fairly easy to figure out how to communicate messages to different groups.

In the Hilton example, lower-paid employees are most concerned about their ability to feed and protect themselves and their families. They couldn't care less about how the stock price will be affected, thus making "management" richer or poorer. They do care about whether their health care benefits will change, and if this means they can or cannot get a raise.

Perspective: Seeing Things from Your Audience's Point of View

Rob and his family were on vacation in sunny Florida. While they were gone, Rob's brother Chad was taking care of their elderly mother. Having been gone for a week, Rob called home to check on how things were going.

"Hey, Chad, how's it going?"

"Well, your cat died."

"What?!" cried Rob.

"Your cat fell off the roof and died," said Chad.

"My god, man, that's a terrible way to break such awful news to me. You could have prepared me for the shock. Why didn't you say, 'Rob, we've had a bit of a problem here. Fluffy ran out of the house and climbed up on the roof. We couldn't get her down. I called the fire department, and they came with their hook and ladder. Before they could reach Fluffy she jumped. Her injuries appeared pretty serious, so we took her to the vet. Even though they tried and tried, they couldn't save her.' Now, doesn't that seem more considerate than just blurting out 'Your cat died'?"

Chad was quiet for a moment. "I guess you're right. I'm sorry."

Rob said, "That's okay. Now, how's Mom?"

"Well, Mom was up on the roof . . . "

Communication is a very messy business. I plugged the word *communication* into the Amazon.com search window and it gave me 168,147 books on that single topic, plus offered me other books on topics such as "effective communication" and "interpersonal communication." I suspect communication must be among the top five book topics in the world, just after sex, food, childcare, and religion.

The reason communication is messy and often studied is that there are so many ways to combine the words we use, so many ways to use our voices to say them, so many expressions we can have on our faces, etc. Now multiply that by the number of filters our audiences have—geographic background, education, family culture, economic strata, and so on. Every one of these filters affects how we send and receive messages.

For an audience to be receptive to a message, it has to hear and understand the message, and also be willing to accept it.

That puts the pressure on the sender of the information to understand where the audience is "coming from."

The Subject Is "You"

No matter what news you deliver, the first question people will consider is "How does this affect me?" Because everyone first wants to understand whether it's good or bad news *from their point of view,* they are unlikely to hear anything you say until they figure out how the news affects their own situation.

Until my daughter was 25, I did not understand how the system worked. She knew exactly how to get me—what I worried about, what made me feel guilty, what made me feel happy and sad, and how far she could go before I put my foot down.

I couldn't understand how I frequently succumbed to her wily ways. Then I had grandchildren, and the patterns became obvious. My vision is now clearer because I don't have the full-time responsibility for molding their little brains, so I can willingly accommodate their every whim. In fact, I rather enjoy watching them manipulate and maneuver me. Like when my granddaughter snuggles up on my lap, looks up lovingly, and says, "Grandma, I want to stay up late so I can spend more time with you." The key phrase here is *so I can spend more time with you.* (So sue me; we all have egos.) Forget college. This child has already earned her MBA in marketing. She has mastered the concept of appealing to others' needs. In this case, the need is love.

From a detached, nonparental standpoint, it's obvious what kids are doing. It's not quite so easy for my poor daughter. Like most new parents, she was ignorant to the fact that a child's first priority is to assess the market.

Children learn early and well that understanding Mommy and Daddy's needs is key. By looking at the bags under his parents' eyes and listening to their crankiness, the baby can see that his parents' need for sleep is paramount. Thus, he can get almost anything he wants if he repeatedly disturbs their sleep, especially if he communicates with them loudly just as they are entering REM sleep.

From crib to college, at each stage of development, a child will uncover new ways to get attention and convert his parents to his way of thinking. Of course, parents use guilt as a weapon to combat this manipulation. "You never call. You never write. Don't you love your mother?"

This is the most common and blatant example I know of in which one person identifies the other's needs and delivers the message in a way that gets action. Now, just apply that same intuitive thinking to your employees. Put yourself in their shoes and think how they must feel about what's happening. But don't rely solely on your empathetic powers to define it. Ask.

DEALING WITH GOOD NEWS AND BAD NEWS

In a company that's committed to great communication, good news and bad news are treated with equal importance. When there are layoffs, management acts with seriousness and concern. When the company wins a customer service award, management acts with enthusiasm and joy.

Let's talk first about good news and what to do with it because few companies take maximum advantage of good news. The stock hits an all-time high and the president sends an e-mail congratulating everyone. Big whoop. Few people will get very excited about an e-mail. If you don't act like this is *big* news, it isn't. And employees will treat it that way.

On the other hand, think what you can accomplish when you shout from the rooftops about what a great thing has happened. Not because "the company" did something outstanding, and not because management led the company to success. This is the time to give all the credit to the employees. What a chance to tell people how much you appreciate them and the job they do. Pull out all the stops. Have a party. Send each person a thank-you note. Put an ad in the paper telling the world how fabulous your employees are. Name names and use photos. Every company can build confidence and gain followers by shouting about employees' successes. Just imagine how proud each person will be as their name is called, or their picture appears in your town's newspaper, or when you congratulate them in front of their families. This sort of recognition earns you points not only with the employee, but also with his or her friends and family. So when you have good news to share, say it loud, say it repeatedly, say it blatantly, and tell it to as many people as you can in as many ways as possible. Spread the credit for the good news around and you'll not only build pride for your company and its employees, you'll also gain their greater commitment.

Good news comes in all sizes. Small wins become big wins, and big wins become monumental wins. It's all in how you treat them.

The flip side, which is much less fun, is how to treat bad news. Bad news is like sauerkraut: If you keep it in the can, the odor will stay strong. Open the can, and the smell eventually will diminish.

No good can come from a head-in-the-sand approach to bad news; just because you don't talk about it doesn't mean no one knows. There are many reasons that management tends to keep bad news under wraps. In a few cases it's appropriate, such as in a serious legal situation. But here is the most important thing to remember about news in your company: Nine times out of ten, employees already know the news before the official word comes out.

When you are secretive about bad news, negative things happen:

- Employees suspect things are worse than they are.
- The grapevine runs rampant with partial or incorrect information.
- Employees lose trust for management.
- Employees become fearful and begin to consider other options, such as alternative employment.

- Employees become less productive, because they spend their time speculating about the bad news and when it will be announced. Some become paralyzed by the unknown.

Rather than being a no-win situation, communicating bad news properly can actually build employees' respect for management and commitment to the company.

A Few Suggestions for Communicating Bad News

When you have bad news to share, follow these guidelines:

- Prepare scripted remarks or create a printed statement and follow it.
- Tell people as many facts as possible without getting into too much detail. For example, in announcing a corporate headquarters move, tell when it will happen, how each group will be affected, what are the next steps. Although people need to know why, the more important topic for this initial announcement is, "What will happen to me?"
- Don't try to "get off the hook" by telling people why the company is justified in its actions. This meeting is not about you; it's about people who make up your company.

Everyone knows that bad things happen sometimes. But if you can openly and honestly tell people what is going to happen, they will respect your honesty and potentially support your efforts. In fact, when the dust settles, you will probably have more trust from employees than ever. They'll know you have been up front and treated them like adults.

STEP 5: MATCH VEHICLES TO THE MESSAGE

Many of our client engagements begin with this statement: We need you to help us create a newsletter. This is a cry in the night. The client knows he needs better or more communication, and the most familiar way he knows to do that is to put out a newsletter. In a few cases, that's exactly what the client needs. More than likely, however, more communication doesn't necessarily mean better communication. To a naked person in a snowstorm, a bikini is "more" clothing, but not exactly "better" clothing.

So our response to the newsletter request is, "Tell me what you need to accomplish." By the time the client finishes relating the situation and the desired result, the solution probably will be somewhat obvious. Once you find out what's right, wrong, or missing, you can match the prescription to the pain.

Advertising guru Fairfax Cone said, "Advertising is what you do when you can't go see someone." The same holds true for internal marketing. If a manager anywhere up the line wants to communicate with anyone else, the best way is generally in person, one on one. Practically speaking, that can happen when a manager has an audience that is a manageable (no pun intended) size. In smaller companies, the president can actually have meetings with all employees at one time.

When the audience outgrows an intimate setting, there are a couple of ways to reach people. In most situations, the supervisor is the best person to relay information. The supervisor is the person who is closest to the situation, knows and understands the people involved, and has the best chance of knowing how to approach them.

When the message is something you feel is best communicated by a person in a higher position, you can use a host of vehicles. But according to Dr. Denison, "It is a mistake for senior leaders to assume that their direct reports will pass along the right message to their direct reports, and so on down the line. . . .

On a rational level, repetition helps everyone understand what they are supposed to do. On an emotional level, it reinforces the human need to bond and be a part of a group."

Frequently, leaders target just their lieutenants to receive regular information about the company's goals. In a healthy company, this might be effective most of the time. In a company where communication has been lacking or trust is an issue, this can be a fatal mistake.

Keeping all of these factors in mind, you will have to make a decision on your own about what will work in your company. Remember, the best advice is just someone else's opinion. When it comes to your own employees, you are the best judge.

Appeal to the Right "Learning Channel"

As you're considering which vehicle best suits the message, take into consideration that people receive information and learn in different ways. Some "hear" best through the spoken word. Others prefer something in print that they can reread. A third type may need a visual approach such as a video or a teleconference. Most people learn more effectively when several of their senses are engaged rather than just one. Choose a variety of media that target the senses and learning styles of all your employees. This will help tailor your messages to each of your employees, and it will also reinforce the messages by repeating them in several different ways. The end result is that the best communication consists of multiple media that reinforce each other.

Advertisers use television, radio, print, billboards, and other media to get their message to consumers. Likewise, an effective internal branding campaign should take advantage of multiple media, and appeal to multiple senses, to reinforce its messages.

Visual media will probably account for most of your brand marketing, because they comprise the most readily available channels. You may want to use a variety of visual media, such as newsletters, e-mails, intranets, posters, and even internal television networks, to reinforce your internal logo and written slogans.

Auditory media is usually the second choice of marketers, because these vehicles are also readily available and can create powerful associations in people's minds. Think of auditory branding like the Intel chime, NBC's three tones, and countless commercial jingles. Music has incredible emotional impact and, used in a marketing capacity, can be extremely powerful, especially when used in tandem with a visual brand. I mentioned before Coca-Cola's "I'd like to buy the world a Coke" campaign. The song came out 30 years ago. I can still sing it today, and when I think of it, I still get a good feeling about Coke.

Human memory is better linked to our olfactory sense than any other, although smell is usually quite difficult to use in branding. I'm reminded, though, of Debbi Fields and her early marketing plan for Mrs. Fields cookies. All she had to do was open the door to her store, where the fresh cookies were baking, and the customers just poured in. There is nothing like the smell of a good old chocolate chip cookie to keep 'em coming back.

Likewise, your employees' taste buds might just be the way to their hearts. But it's not as easy to brand your company using taste. (Unless you're Mrs. Fields, in which case you've got smell *and* taste going for you.) Again, with a cookie example, at Doubletree hotels, guests are given a warm, freshly baked cookie when they check in. The cookies are meant for the guests, of course, but they have the added benefit of making Doubletree one of the most delicious-smelling places to work outside of the food industry (and we would be amazed if employees didn't sneak a cookie every once in a while as well). Internally, the company has used the cookie to denote its care for guests. In fact, it has a CARE committee to keep guests' needs uppermost in employees' minds. And a couple of years ago, the company designed the cover of its annual brand marketing plan to look like the texture of a cookie.

WHICH VEHICLES FOR WHICH INFORMATION?

There's etiquette when it comes to communication. There are certain things you communicate over certain media, and certain things you simply don't. For instance, while you might shoot off a quick e-mail to a friend you haven't spoken to in a while, you do not break up with your significant other via e-mail (although we know people who have, and we are appalled).

The same is true in corporate communications. Some communication vehicles are more appropriate for some messages than others. Fortunately for you, we're here to help you sort them out.

So what kind of vehicles fit what kind of information? Here are some of the types of communications you may deliver:

- Mission, vision, and values
- Motivational information
- Strategic information
- Recognition of team members' accomplishments
- Company news
- Financial information
- Detailed factual information
- Detailed training
- Management directives

In each case, ask yourself what you want people to do with the information.

Mission, Vision, and Values

A couple years ago, IBM did something rather extraordinary. IBM management decided they wanted to evolve their corporate values, and instead of sitting in a room by themselves, they asked all of their employees at every level in the organization to sit down with them and define their corporate values together.

Involving employees in a values-definition exercise isn't so unusual . . . unless you have 330,000 employees. They would have to find a pretty big room to hold that meeting, and they did—the Internet (or more precisely, IBM's intranet).

"We want our employees to be involved in the business we build," says Mike Hill, general manager of IBM's telecommunications industry. "Sam [Palmisano] wanted to create a unified set of values of being an IBMer . . . and he sent the message to everyone at IBM that he wanted their help to develop them."

IBM threw one of the biggest parties of all time. They called it "World Jam," reminiscent of an impromptu gathering of talented people to create something beautiful together (although the technology behind such a feat was anything but impromptu—IBM just has a way of making impossible things look effortless).

Their intranet played host for 72 hours to the more than 50,000 employees who showed up. They offered over 6,000 ideas for IBM's corporate values change, and IBM's technology worked in the background to distill all that information into the most common themes.

When the party was over, IBM management presented the three values that best reflected the thousands of ideas their employees had shared, and they asked for their employees' feedback again. When Sam Palmisano sent out the final results, he knew that they had succeeded in developing a set of values that truly represented the company. Mike Hill says this about the Jam:

> IBMers by the tens of thousands weighed in. They were thoughtful and passionate about the company they want to be a part of. They were also brutally honest. Some of what they wrote was painful to read, because they pointed out all the bureaucratic and dysfunctional things that get in the way of serving clients, working as a team, or implementing new ideas. But we were resolute in keeping the di-

alog free-flowing and candid. And I don't think what resulted—broad, enthusiastic, grass-roots consensus—could have been obtained in any other way.

We believe that a company's mission, vision, and values (MVVs) are among the most important things you can ever communicate to your employees. If you are just developing or revamping your mission, vision, or values, we highly recommend that you solicit input from your employees to involve them, as IBM did. It's a powerful way of creating a sense of ownership in the organization and showing your employees that you value their opinions. It is certainly the easiest and surest way to make sure your employees know your MVVs because they wrote them!

If your MVVs are already established, make sure you imbed them in every interaction with your employees—in every communication, in training and orientation, and, of course, in your management decisions and actions. They should be communicated in every media as often as possible until they are ingrained in every employee's mind.

A company's values, and to some extent its mission and vision as well, should be reviewed every so often to make sure they still reflect the company and the world around it. IBM continues to host World Jam sessions every year on multiple topics, one of which is to make sure its values still hold relevance for its employees and business practices. That's what we call a best practice!

Motivational Information

Do you want your employees to be motivated by your message? Motivational information is best delivered by a person, in person, so the audience can see and feel the speaker's enthusiasm, see his body language and hear his voice and inflections. The next best way is to deliver it over a Webcast, where you have the advantage of being live where your employees can still see and hear the person, even if they aren't in the same room. Your employees can also replay a Webcast if they didn't have a chance to attend the original session. A third choice is a phone conference, because it too is "live." Video would be a fourth choice, though it lacks spontaneity, an important part of motivation. However, video does allow you to see the speaker's excitement. Print should be used as a last resort because it doesn't have the human element.

Strategic Information

If your message involves strategic information, it's probably important information, so you'll want to make sure your audiences thoroughly understand it. Strategic information includes things such as the launch of a new initiative, new goals, the announcement of a merger, or other major decisions that affect the whole company or a major portion of the staff.

In these kinds of cases, you'll probably want to utilize more than one medium to make sure you get the message across. You may first want to announce it in person, such as at an all-hands meeting. Live and in person is the best way to go for strategic announcements for the same reasons that applied to motivational information.

After the announcement, you should follow up quickly with more details about the new strategy/decision, including things that employees need to know and do to be successful. See the "Management Directive" and "Detailed Factual Information" sections for more ideas, and use a combination of vehicles that seems appropriate for the kind of strategic information you're communicating.

Recognition of Team Members' Accomplishments

Remember what we said about good news? You've got to shout it from the rooftops. Well, recognizing your team members is good news you can create anytime, all the time. Grab a ladder, grab a megaphone, and start belting it out.

There are lots of ways of recognizing people, and we recommend throwing caution to the wind and trying a few different approaches. Remember that one man's recognition is another man's paparazzi, so keep your employees' preferences in mind when you recognize them. It may be a good idea to ask your employees how they would like to be recognized.

Different levels of heroics deserve different kinds of recognition. There's the "we know you work hard every day" recognition and then there's the "you just performed mission impossible for the company" recognition. The smaller jobs can be awarded with a heartfelt e-mail (private and/or public), displaying their pictures in the company newsletter, or adding their name to the company's Employee of the Month plaque.

The "mission impossible" job deserves something special—a personal thank you from the CEO in front of the rest of the company, an award presented at the next all-staff meeting, or a small, spontaneous party with balloons and cake (or beer and wine) just for that special person or team.

Don't overlook opportunities to call out a few names during staff meetings or company conference calls, or in newsletters and other regular communications. Whenever possible, give the thanks in person as well as through other media.

There are, of course, financial awards and gifts, which we encourage you to give as well, if you can, but keep in mind that feeling recognized is an emotional thing and sometimes your employees just want a sincere pat on the back and a thank you.

Company News

Do you have good news or bad news to deliver? Is it big news or small news? Far too many of our corporate brethren seem intent on only communicating one kind of news—big bad news. We're here to tell you that just ain't right. If you communicate honestly, clearly, and often with your employees, no matter what the news, they will trust and love you.

If the news is big and good (such as a successful launch of a new product or service, soaring stock price due to a bumper year, or Steve Jobs agreeing to join as the chief marketing officer), again, get out the megaphone. Make a big deal out of it, and do it in color. Follow the formula for motivational information—do it live and in person, if possible, or by phone or Webcast.

If the news is big and bad (such as layoffs, a merger, a takeover, or something with negative legal ramifications), then announce it quickly and honestly and look for the silver lining. Employees appreciate honesty. Even if you have bad news to share, it's better to tell them right away rather than sugarcoat it. Many leaders have been surprised and gratified by grateful, if not happy, responses they have received to bad news when they have communicated it with integrity.

You probably won't be able to tell everyone in person, but you should deliver this kind of news in a "sympathetic" medium. A conference call or Webcast is a good medium because each offers the opportunity for people to ask questions if they choose, but you should always filter the questions ahead of time to make sure they are appropriate. A handwritten letter is also an acceptable medium, but e-mail should be avoided in this case because it's too casual.

For smaller good news (such as hitting a deadline, accomplishing a small goal, or positive changes to benefits), make it seem bigger than it is. Usually that means taking the medium you were going to use and stepping it up a level. If you were going to send out an e-mail, use voicemail instead. If you were going to print it in the company newsletter, bring it up in the all-staff meeting instead.

For smaller bad news (such as loss of a client or account, an employee departure, or negative changes to benefits), it's okay to put these nuggets in print (usually an e-mail or newsletter). Go ahead and find the silver lining and surround the bad news with good news. You're letting the troops know that you lost a battle, but you're still winning the war.

Financial Information

Financial information can be sensitive, so handle with care. We recommend print media because it's just too difficult to absorb the numbers otherwise. When we were working with Hampton Inn, we had to send out the financial implications of the initiative to all the hotel franchise owners, and we chose to do it as a nicely designed packet with an accompanying letter. Choose a letter or booklet over e-mail for sensitive information, because it minimizes the possibility that the information will get into the wrong hands.

Detailed Factual Information

Whenever you want people to be able to study information carefully or to keep it as a reference, print is a good way to go. Nothing beats being able to hold information in your hands and look it over carefully. If the information has columns with numbers, some people like to get out the old ruler to make sure they're viewing the correct lines.

Any type of detailed information such as training, directions, or financial information should be in print. Some people don't grasp things of this nature unless they can pore over it for a while. All this detail should be preceded with an overview that explains the information, to give meaning to the dry details. You may choose to deliver this in another medium first and then reiterate it in print, as context for the detailed information.

Detailed Training

Training can be conducted in several different media, depending on the nature of the material. We've developed classroom training, detailed workbook training, DVD and audio training, and interactive training, and we recently helped develop a training program using that latest of crazes, the Learning Map.

Management Directives

When management needs to drive change in the organization, they may issue a management directive. It's a call to action, a signal to the troops that they need to step up and support the change. The communication you utilize to build weight and momentum behind a directive needs to be clear, motivating, and ubiquitous. You can borrow the strategies from the "Strategic Information," "Motivational Information," and "Company News" sections to help you get the message across, depending on the kind of directive and change.

HOW TO MAKE THE MOST OF YOUR COMMUNICATION VEHICLES

Now that we know what types of information you may need to communicate to your employees, it is time to determine which vehicles to use to get the message across effectively. Figure 5.1 provides an overview of the communication vehicles that are best suited to delivering the variety of messages discussed above.

Company Meeting

Going to a live company meeting is kind of like going to a rock concert. You get the full experience. You can see, hear, smell, and taste the excitement and energy in the room. That's why it should be your top choice for any really important information you have to deliver—anything strategic, a big news announcement, etc. It's also the best place to deliver motivational information and give recognition to people who have really helped the company.

Here are some things to keep in mind about live company or departmental meetings:

- Be bright, be loud, and be bigger than life. If it's your annual meeting, throw out all the stops, hire a band, drop con-

fetti from the ceiling—make it *fun* for your employees. If they only get to see all their colleagues and leadership in the same room one day a year, you've got to remind them why they want to work for you the other 364 days of the year.
- Get senior leadership up on stage as much as possible. The top executives are the celebrities of your company. If you've been doing a good job of internal marketing, hopefully everyone knows, loves, and respects your fearless leaders, so any message from them will carry the right kind of weight. If your senior leadership isn't well loved, we recommend that you lock them in a room with this book, a puppy, and some milk and cookies so they can get in touch with what's really important in life.
- Speak from the heart, not a PowerPoint slide or script. (See the PowerPoint discussion later in this chapter.)
- For smaller, departmental or regional meetings, still make a big deal of them. You're there to communicate with your employees, and as such, you're representing the company. All the same principles apply. You wouldn't air a really dry, lackluster advertisement just because it was on a regional station instead of a national station, so don't hold a meeting that's utterly boring for people to sit through either. If you're the head of a department or region, try to get your team together at least a couple times a year to share company news and industry developments, and especially to recognize your team. It's important to the cohesiveness of your group. Make sure you give them something exciting to look forward to when you do.

Videoconference/Web Conference

Videoconferencing is the next best alternative to a real live meeting. Videoconferencing and Web conferencing are huge assets to companies that are far-flung geographically, because they give you the opportunity to hold a "live" company meeting without the expense of flying everyone to the same spot.

Videoconferences and Web conferences also have the advantage of being recordable media, so you're also not limited by people's schedules. If employees have another meeting to attend or are busy working during the time of the meeting, they always have the opportunity to replay it.

Here are some tips for videoconferences and Web conferences:

- Video can be a bit intimidating, and it's normal for people to freeze up in front of the camera, unless they happen to have done a stint in Hollywood. Make sure the speaker has a chance to rehearse (especially if it's a live presentation), and replay some practice shots until she gets into a natural, comfortable pace. Your audience will be much more comfortable watching someone with natural, easy body language than a stiff plank of wood.
- If you're doing a Web conference with a speaker, the same rules apply, but if you're conducting a Web conference in which you're displaying a presentation, follow the rules regarding good PowerPoint etiquette discussed later in this chapter.
- If you're conducting a Web conference, make sure you allow some time at the end for people to ask questions. Many Web conference services have a moderator—either a live person or a technical moderator built into the system—that will screen questions so you can feel assured that you won't be embarrassed with questions that are inappropriate.

Business TV

Business TV has become a hot medium in the last decade or so. It's basically television programming that is about your company, made by and for people in your company. Many companies have Business TV streaming 24/7 on a never-ending loop, providing their employees with company news, stock information, benefits, new product/service information, industry info, you name it. A lot of companies that have a large number employees or offices all over the map, such as FedEx and The Home Depot, use Business TV to keep their employees informed and in tune with the company.

Here are some rules for the effective use of Business TV:

- Content must be innovative, fresh, targeted, and diversified.
- If possible, content should be interactive (polls, quizzes, surveys) to engage the audience. This also makes Business TV a great vehicle for soliciting feedback from your employees.
- Mix it up. We've seen successful Business TV programs that look a little like CNN. At any given time there are several things going on—a center image with the main story, stock ticker at the bottom of the screen, and maybe weather information and bulleted news off in a side panel. We're in the age of media overload, and you'll have to join the crowd if you want to keep employees' attention.

Conference Calls

A companywide or departmentwide conference call is a good way to deliver an important message if you can't gather the troops in one location for a meeting, and if you don't have videoconferencing or Web conferencing capabilities. The disembodied voice of your fearless leader is a better alternative than print media if you need to convey motivational information.

Keep the following in mind as you plan your call:

- Your audience doesn't have anything to look at when they're on a conference call, so it's often difficult to concentrate on what the speaker is saying, and it's almost impossible for them to retain detailed information. For this

reason, we recommend that conference call scripts be kept light and conversational so your audience will have an easier time following the conversation.
- Just as with videoconferences and Web conferences, leave some time at the end of the call for people to ask questions. Have a moderator take questions offline and coordinate the Q&A session.
- Always follow up your conference call with an e-mail recapping the highlights of the call, any important information your audience needs to remember, and any actions you need people to take. Record the call if you can, so that people who couldn't tune in for the live call can listen to it later.

Print Piece/Letter

There's something antiquated and nostalgic about receiving a real letter in the mail. Maybe that's why it gets people's attention. It's easy to ignore an e-mail, but when you have a letter addressed to you in your hands, well, there's something irresistible about it.

That's why print pieces and letters are our top media choices for *following up* on really important issues (which should always be announced first in person or at least via a videoconference/web conference or a conference call).

Here are a few things we've learned about print pieces and letters:

- Personalize it. If it's a letter, make sure the receiver's name is on it. If it's a preprinted pamphlet or brochure, accompany it with a short letter that has the receiver's name on it. If you don't personalize the letter, it might still end up in the junk mail pile.
- Make it colorful and professional looking. If it's a letter, print it on your letterhead, in color, and make sure it has a digital signature at the bottom. It gives it that "I wrote this just for you" feeling. If it's a print piece, make it glossy, col-

orful, and sexy. Of course, always match the design to the occasion. If you're communicating sensitive information or bad news, keep it conservative and professional. If it's good news, make it sparkle and shine.

Newsletters

Newsletters have to be one of the most insidious communication devices ever put on this earth. Sorry, but that's how they are usually utilized. We probably could have written a book just on this one topic, but we'll exercise restraint. Here are our thoughts for putting together a snazzier and more reader-friendly newsletter:

- Make it fun! If it isn't enjoyable to read, it won't be read. Include fun stories, interesting facts, jokes, and quizzes. In one newsletter we put together recently, we included a quiz about our colleagues' past jobs. Everyone was roaring with laughter when they found out that our COO used to be an actor at a dinner theatre, and one of our managers used to tend the garden at a graveyard. Yikes! How did these people ever break into the business world?
- Mix it up. Most companies do a good job of including a diverse mix of information in their newsletters, but we thought we should mention it anyway. Keep doing it. It keeps the newsletters interesting. Include company and industry news, a little blurb from the CEO, birthdays, etc.—and don't forget to include plenty of fun stuff.
- Feature different "voices." If the newsletter only features the voice of corporate headquarters, guess what? People in corporate headquarters might be the only ones who care to read it. Instead, solicit quotes, opinions, stories, etc., from other people in the company. If it feels like everyone in the company had a hand in it, more people will be interested in reading it.

- Recognize people. In our opinion, just about every medium is a good medium for recognizing people, and this is one of them. There's something about seeing your name in print that makes people all giddy inside.

E-mail

Did we say that newsletters were the most insidious communication medium on earth? Sorry, e-mail is worse.

E-mail is the Honda Civic of information vehicles. It is the most used and most ignored channel through which you can communicate with your employees. We're not telling you not to use it, but we do recommend that you use it less than you probably already do. Whenever possible, substitute one of the other communication vehicles in favor of e-mail. Here are a few cases where it *is* appropriate to use e-mail:

- When you are sending an invitation to a meeting or a call, or to alert people of updated intranet content, an online survey, etc., then e-mail is a great way to "push" information to your audience that will cause them to seek out other media sources.
- E-mail is a good way to distribute quick, small bits of company news that are time-sensitive or that you want to make sure everyone sees (otherwise, it can go onto the company intranet or in a newsletter). E-mail is *not* meant for communicating extensive amounts of information, detailed training, important and strategic information, really bad news, really good news, or just about anything else of substance. Save it for a vehicle with more horsepower.

Now that we know *when* it's appropriate to use e-mail, let's go over some e-mail etiquette:

- Keep it brief and targeted. People receive e-mail all day long. They will not spend time reading a long e-mail from corporate headquarters.
- Build your brand through e-mail. If your e-mail system supports HTML, use your company colors and logo to help create a branded communication. E-mail is a great opportunity to reinforce your internal brand, although few companies take advantage of it.
- Don't send anything sensitive through e-mail. We have to add a disclaimer here: We believe very strongly in creating a culture of trust in your organization, and everything we talk about in this book is designed to do just that. But it is also a company's responsibility to protect its assets and make sure they aren't abused. Therefore, we recommend that you don't send sensitive information via e-mail, unless you have an e-mail system that allows you to control the privacy of that information. Some e-mail systems (such as Lotus Notes) can prevent e-mail recipients from forwarding or copying e-mails, but if your e-mail system doesn't do this, it's easy for employees to forward confidential information to other people if it's in an electronic format.

Intranet

Intranets have become one of the most popular corporate communication tools for companies of all sizes, and in recent years they have become much more.

IBM is the proud owner of what is probably the most powerful intranet in the world. It's called the On Demand Workplace, and is fondly nicknamed W3.

W3 reaches every single one of IBM's 330,000 employees and 50,000 contractors around the world, and it can be completely personalized for each of them to show geographic, industry, role-specific, and individual-specific information. An IBMer can log in from anywhere in the world and have everything he needs at his fingertips. Pretty cool, huh?

When Sam Palmisano, IBM's chairman, wants to send a letter to IBM employees, it's a flick of his wrist, and 380,000 people have a personalized letter, addressed to them, on their computer desktop. (In addition to that, IBM encourages its employees to e-mail the chairman directly, and he reads and responds to his own mail. We're impressed.)

Like most companies, IBM used to have trouble competing with the folks at the water cooler. Most employees used to trust their peers more than the corporate communication mumbo jumbo coming at them. But IBM conducted a survey recently, and found that employees now consider the corporate intranet to be the most trusted source of information. "And right in the top middle of that screen is the corporate message," says Alex Herrmann, global communications lead for IBM's communications sector. That's powerful stuff.

Chances are your company doesn't have quite as big a budget or as many resources at your disposal (W3 is, of course, built entirely on IBM's own technology). But you can still turn your intranet into a dynamic and powerful communication vehicle. It is an ideal vehicle for communicating follow-up information after a company meeting or announcement, and the number one place to archive all communications and just about every piece of information about your company and industry for employees to do their one-stop business literacy shopping. It is also the ideal address for measurement surveys and other forms of feedback. And one more thought: IBM put a comprehensive training program on their intranet (just about every kind of training on every topic you can possibly imagine), and saved $300 million in one year just on its training expenses. All those smart people at IBM just got a little bit smarter.

One on One

If going to a company meeting is like going to a rock concert, then having a one-on-one dialogue with your employees is like giving them VIP backstage passes.

One-on-one communication is the number one choice for more personal kinds of communication, like performance management feedback, discussing an employee's career goals, and soliciting feedback from employees. Sensitive communications, such as the need to lay off someone, should *always* take place in person.

The one-on-one interactions we're talking about usually take place between an employee and his direct supervisor in those situations in which the supervisor is acting on behalf of the company, so she is the vehicle for corporate communication.

Of course, it's important to be sensitive about people's feelings in any discussion about personal goals, performance, and feedback. Let's consider the following scenario:

Jill: "Barbara, your performance sucks."
Barbara: "Ouch, Jill. That kind of hurt my feelings."
Jill: "Wimp."

This obviously isn't an ideal performance management review. In situations such as this, a manager is acting as an ambassador of the company, so it's important that managers communicate with their employees in a sensitive, caring way.

Done right, one-one-one communication can be the most powerful communication vehicle at your disposal. That's one of the reasons we recommend providing good training to your employees, so they have the right attitude and skills to be positive ambassadors for the company.

Bulletin Boards

Bulletin boards fall into a whole category of communications vehicles that today's managers overlook completely. They're not sexy. They're not interactive. They're not "now." But they work. Although bulletin boards didn't make our top ten communications vehicles list, there is a place for these rather rudimentary tools.

I suppose I have an emotional attachment to bulletin boards, because in my first job I was responsible for a bulletin board system. I had the pleasure of preparing information for our bulletin boards, such as the menus of the week, which I think I gave a clever name like Food Fare or some other alliterative title. The boards resided in 14 locations in seven or eight buildings. Every Friday, I walked to each location with my 14 identical sets of postings and my box of pushpins. I digress.

Bulletin boards are perfect for posting announcements, pictures of employees of the month, and menus, as well as legal documents that are required to be displayed in a public place. Use them for information that's short and sweet, so that even a person passing by can get the gist of what's there.

Unusual Means of Sharing

Soon we all may use a form of communication we haven't used before—phone messages. One of our more communicative and animated clients will record a message to greet participants at a conference. They'll be alerted to the message when they arrive in their hotel rooms and can retrieve it whenever they choose. It's a little extra welcome touch that personalizes their conference experience.

Another truly innovative means of communication is a posting on the inside of a bathroom stall. We don't necessarily endorse this vehicle for communication unless you're advertising a company health program. Somehow we just don't envision employees reading about the new benefits policy at this point during their day.

AND NOW A WORD ABOUT POWERPOINT

We admit it. This section is about a pet peeve. It's a personal thing. It's something to which we probably overreact. And it's a subject to which we've probably given more time than it deserves. But it means a lot to us. And when you become an author, you can stress things that get your goat.

In the old days, we supported our presentations with glassine slides. To clean smudges off the glass we wore special white cotton gloves. When the slides had dust or lint on them, we blew it off using an aerosol can containing air under high pressure. When they were ready to be shown, we loaded them into a carousel that advanced noisily as we projected the images on a screen. It sounds medieval now, and there's no question that it was torture putting them together. A time-consuming process, it required that you have your final presentation finished well in advance of when you had to deliver it. (Was that really a bad thing?)

Through the miracle of technology, we don't have to fiddle with slides now. Instead, we whip up a presentation on our computers, most often using a software program called Microsoft PowerPoint. Undoubtedly, there are other programs similar to the Microsoft version. If so, I don't know them by name. That's because the name PowerPoint has become almost a generic term for presentations. (Because this book is all about branding, we respect the PowerPoint name. But because we always use the PowerPoint software, we also refer to it here as a generic presentation vehicle.)

Yes, PowerPoint is cheaper, faster, and sometimes more accurate than the old-fashioned slides. But it is also leading to the downfall of mankind as we know it. From what I can tell, less than one-thousandth of one percent of the population understands the purpose of a slide. So here are our rules for creating an effective PowerPoint presentation.

PowerPoint screens are supposed to:

- Support a presentation by giving the audience a quick outline of what the speaker is saying. This helps the audience organize the speaker's ideas so they don't have to work too hard to get the gist of the material the speaker is presenting. And remember, we said that people retain information best if they hear it and see it.
- Be easy to change so that you can catch errors or change thoughts even minutes before you present.
- Be shown via your computer, eliminating the need for hard slides and the accompanying projection equipment.
- Make it easy to print handouts for the audience.

PowerPoint was not designed to:

- Be a crutch for the speaker. No speaker should ever look over his or her shoulder at the slides. The slides are for the audience, not the speaker. Anyone who is presenting should know the information well enough that if the computer suddenly crashes, they can still deliver the information flawlessly. (And get real—it *has* happened.)
- Contain every word of the speaker's presentation. Screens should be simple and easy to read. The rule for making slides is they should contain no more than six bullets each, and no more than six words per bullet. This is absolute heresy to the people who insist on putting entire paragraphs one after another on a single slide.
- Show more than a handful of numbers. No Microsoft Excel spreadsheet should ever appear on a PowerPoint screen. Detailed information belongs in a handout. Slides should summarize and reinforce the key points. When a slide has too many numbers, the audience doesn't know what to look at. A slide should point out the important information.

The last, most important point we will share regarding PowerPoint is never, never, never use the color red for your text. It blurs the type and makes your audience think it's time for an eye exam. That's certainly not the way to clear communications.

READY, SET, NO NOT YET

You're more than halfway there. You've completed Steps 1 through 5, so you know your environment and your audiences, you've evaluated the receptiveness of your audiences, you've defined your key communications principles and messages, and you've carefully matched your media to your audiences.

Your moment is about to arrive. After just one more chapter, you will have completed all eight steps. So hang in there for just a handful of pages and you'll be ready to strike that match.

FIGURE 5.1 Matching Communication Messages with Effective Vehicles

Communication Vehicles

DB2	Company Meeting	Video/Web Conference	Business TV	Conference Call	Print Piece/Letter	Newsletters	E-mail	Intranet	One-on-One
Mission, Vision, and Values	◁	◁			♦	♦	♦	♦	♦
Motivational Information	◁	◁						♦	♦
Strategic Information	◁	◁			♦	♦		♦	♦
Recognizing People	◁	◁			♦	♦	♦	♦	◁
Company News	◁	◁	◁			◁		◁	
Financial Information					◁			♦	
Tactical Plans		◁			◁		◁	◁	
Detailed Training		◁						◁	
Management Directives	◁	◁		◁	♦	♦		♦	♦

Type of Communication

Primary Communication Vehicles ♦
Follow-up Communication Vehicles ◁

Chapter 6

A MATCH, A ZIPPO, OR A BLOWTORCH

If you've followed all the steps carefully, you won't have to resort to rubbing two sticks together to get your fire going. You have much more powerful tools for getting your employees excited, aligned, and ready to do what's necessary to emblazon your brand on the hearts and minds of your customers.

So far, we've looked, evaluated, examined, measured, and defined. You name it; we've done all the things so closely associated with planning. Thus, we've covered all the aspects of planning a great internal marketing effort. In this chapter, we'll finally let you get out of the starting gate because now you're ready to win the race.

STEP 6: CHOOSE YOUR CHAMPIONS

There's a name for people who think they can pull off such a grand effort by themselves. We call them megalomaniacs. It's not a pretty word, and it's not a smart strategy. Even small projects benefit from team involvement, and a campaign this big is impossible without help. Eventually, you'll have all your employees engaged, but where do you find help between then and now? You need a champion or two by your side.

A champion is someone who outwardly endorses a cause, who speaks on its behalf, and who becomes personally associated with it in others' minds. Former First Lady Jackie Kennedy was a champion of the arts. Britain's Princess Diana and Paul McCartney's wife, Heather Mills, have both spoken out on land mines. Actor Michael J. Fox and Ron Reagan, son of the late president, speak in favor of stem cell research. Celebrities such as these have the visibility and clout to bring attention and support to worthwhile causes.

Unless you're a member of the Trump organization, you probably don't have such a high-profile person to champion your cause. But you undoubtedly do have people in your company who command respect and exert tremendous influence. These are the leaders who seem to have the power to convince others to support—or to not support—ideas and initiatives.

A champion doesn't necessarily have a big title. Rather, he or she has the ability to sway opinions and rally others to a cause.

Because the whole purpose of your internal marketing process is to enlist allies, it stands to reason that these people could play a key role in the success or failure of your efforts. The smart thing to do is to make sure you have these people on your side at the starting line.

Where to Find a Champion

There are two kinds of champions: formal and informal. A formal champion is someone in a position of power who can make decisions for or against your plan. An informal champion is anyone to whom others go for advice or opinions. Although they may not be able to officially help or hurt your efforts, they can affect how others feel about what you're doing.

Here are people you might want and need as champions:

- The most articulate, enthusiastic, and well-liked executive in your company
- A senior executive who has the ear of the senior-most decision maker
- Leaders who have large groups of employees
- Employees who are well-liked and who generally are outspoken
- Managers who have a vested interest in your plan's success or failure
- People who will be most affected by your plan

The best approach is to get these people on your side in advance. Now let's discuss how to do that.

Getting Champions on Board

There are a few really effective ways to get people to support you, and they're definitely not rocket science. All you need to do is follow these principles.

Be inclusive. By giving people a say, you create ownership. However, you'll have to decide at what point it makes sense to involve others. You don't want management involved until you've carefully thought things through, and you do want employees involved in the development process.

Value everyone's opinion. Listen to ideas and consider every one important. Welcome negative input. If you don't take it into consideration now, you'll hear about it later when you may not be able to do anything about it.

Help people see what's in it for them. Even leaders like to know that there's something positive in store for them as a result of their involvement.

Keep your champions informed at every step of the way. No one wants to be blindsided, and there's no surer way to make a champion disconnect that to embarrass him or her or allow them to be caught off guard.

Consider a spokesperson or a mascot. There are champions like Michael J. Fox, and then there are product-related celebrity spokespersons. Catherine Zeta-Jones comes to mind, having been highly visible during our Elizabeth Arden adventure. I think we're supposed to imagine that if we use the product Catherine endorses, we will magically transform into a woman who has a flawless body, flawless skin, flawless hair, and a husband who, inexplicably, wants to be married to a phenomenal beauty who is a few decades his junior. Go figure.

Model and actress Milla Jovovich touts L'Oreal cosmetics, tennis great Venus Williams represents Reebok International Inc., and comedian Jerry Seinfeld has stumped for American Express. What can they do for a brand? By associating themselves with a brand, they substantially endorse its value and its effectiveness to do what it claims to do (sometimes despite evidence to the contrary).

So what about your brand? Do you need an internal mascot or spokesperson?

First of all, if you have a celebrity spokesperson representing your brand externally, you may indeed want to include them in your internal brand marketing plan. Sprint sponsored champion skier Picabo Street for its Olympic sponsorship, and also had her attend employee events.

Sprint also hired Buck O'Neil, the first African-American to coach a major league baseball team, to represent the spirit of perseverance and achievement for its employees.

Celebrity involvement will cost you, and the level of the celebrity involved will dictate how much. You'll have to decide how valuable the celebrity's involvement could be in helping establish an internal brand.

If you don't have a high-profile spokesperson, you could consider hiring someone who is well-known locally, such as a star basketball player from your university, or a TV personality who would be interesting for your employees to meet.

Finally, if you want to have some fun, create your own mascot or spokesperson. Draw a cartoon and use the character in your presentations or on collateral materials. Or adopt a pet from an animal shelter and give it a good home, a fun name, and lots of new friends to enjoy.

We would like to offer a word of warning, however. When you hire a celebrity to represent your brand, you do so because the power of association with a good name works in your favor. But what happens if the celebrity falls from grace? Celebrities are famous for what they do in public, such as win tennis games, earn Academy Awards, or create empires. What they do in private is irrelevant; that is, unless their private life contains skeletons and the skeletons become public.

Whether a celebrity is actually guilty of something illegal or inappropriate matters very little. The mere reporting of a suspicion leads to a tarnished reputation for the star. We've seen celebrities get dumped from product endorsements overnight when the star's ethics or morals are deemed questionable. Sometimes the problem doesn't even have to directly involve the star. It may be an issue with a family member or friend. Guilt by association exists.

So as you are considering someone to act as your spokesperson, be aware that there could be pitfalls.

STEP 7: NOW, EXECUTE THE PLAN

Carrying out your plan may seem as easy as simply following the steps you've already defined, but there are pitfalls to just putting one foot automatically in front of the other.

No well-ordered plan is static. As you move through the cycle of creating your internal marketing plan, evaluate your progress along the way and consider areas that are working and those that are not. Be aware of things you need to fix or improve, and tweak your plan to keep it vital and relevant.

A plan is only as effective as your follow-through. When you begin, you may be on a tight timetable, but the balance between the quality of your plan and timing is crucial. Don't sacrifice key elements just because you can't meet all those concrete deadlines. If the volume of work seems too great, think about moving some elements to a later date. Don't let yourself get caught in the "gotta do it the way we planned" trap. Not everything is as critically important as you may think. In the most recent initiative we did for a company, we reached a point where plan information was changing so fast that we didn't have time to make every vehicle perfect from the standpoint of graphic design or print. It went against the grain for us, but we knew that getting the information out *soon* was more important than getting the information out "pretty."

It's easy to start easing off the plan as things begin to take shape. "Do we really need to do all that? We've made good progress, so maybe we can just skip that part and save some money." These are famous last words. If it was important enough to include in your original plan, how did it become unimportant now? A slam-dunk kickoff doesn't guarantee ongoing support. You have constituents to maintain, and you need them to be just as enthusiastic midway as they were when you first got them fired up. Communication is still absolutely essential to keeping everyone on board, so keep those two-way channels open. Tell them what you're going to do, tell them what you're doing as you're doing it, tell them what you've done (and make sure you give *them* the credit).

Finally, as you implement, say thank you at least 20 times a day through personal contact, pats on the back (literally), via e-mail, on the phone, in front of others, and so on. Next to communication, recognition is the most important element of a successful implementation. Not only will people help you get this job done, they'll come back to help next time. And they'll like it! In Chapter 9, we'll tell you more about recognizing and rewarding employees.

Do I Have to Eat *All* My Carrots?

Through our consulting experiences we've learned that you sometimes must feed clients small bites of the ideal. We've seldom found a company that was prepared to ditch all its existing communication processes and create the perfect internal marketing program start to finish. In most cases, budget, personnel or time constraints preclude it. What's more, an executive may feel a plan this sweeping is a bit too much of a risk to take all at once. He or she could be willing to try out a piece of the plan and then, based on those results, add other elements.

Can you effectively implement parts of an internal marketing plan? Of course you can. Certainly there are pieces of the plan that must come first. You wouldn't implement vehicles without defining your audiences and their needs. One without the other would be inexact and highly likely to fail. The way to create success is to follow the steps, but on a small scale.

Here's what we mean. It's absolutely essential to complete Steps 1 through 4, the assessment and message portions of the plan. When you arrive at Step 5, choosing your vehicles, you can make some choices. For example, rather than implement a new companywide intranet, how about creating an HTML e-mail that delivers pictures in the body of the e-mail message? It's a step up from a regular text e-mail, so you can show employees the new graphics associated with the internal marketing strategy.

Or, instead of eliminating any current publications you may have, why not revamp them with a new look and approach to your defined messages? Add some recognition elements to the publications. It's a cheap way to start patting people on the back in front of a wide audience.

The point is that you don't have to establish a D-Day to wipe the slate clean. Implementation can be a gradual process.

So What's First?

Is there an official start time? Actually, there doesn't have to be a grand kickoff for your plan. You may decide you want that, but it's not necessary. In fact, in some cases it's best to begin to gradually unveil plans. Authors of novels use a technique called foreshadowing in which they set up a foundation for an event that comes later. For instance, when a character in a suspense novel is known for her rock-climbing ability, there's a good chance that later in the book she'll be called upon to use it, probably in some suspenseful way. Foreshadowing gives people a hint of what's to come so that when it happens it seems perfectly natural.

Knowing that people resist both good and bad change, it helps to prepare them by dropping clues. Mind you, we don't mean being secretive or mysterious about something that's going to happen. This just creates uneasiness and fear. The way to lay the groundwork is by helping people understand that something is going to happen.

For example, if you're about to refine your goals, let people know that a diverse group of employees and managers will meet to talk about how the company can increase its success or enhance customer service or be more innovative. You don't have to tell them that it's going to lead to a sweeping change. Simply include mention of this activity in your regular communications. This will let them see that you're being inclusive in a process, rather than sending a group of executives off to determine the employees' future. See the difference?

Most important as you go through the process is to include employees and to tell people as much as you can about why things are happening. Treat them as adults. They can accept bad news as well as good news. Chances are good that even if you deliver bad news, employees will respect you for your honesty and perhaps become even more committed to helping get the company through tough times.

STEP 8: MEASURE AND ADAPT

If you can measure it, you can manage it. It's somewhat of a no-brainer, eh? How are you going to know your plan is working if you don't use some way of defining an end result and checking to see if you did it? Remember, you created objectives at the beginning of this process. Now is when they come into play. Establish your criteria and measure intermittently throughout your initiative so you can recognize what needs to be tweaked and proactively adjust your plan.

Measuring at the end of the initiative helps you to know what you've accomplished overall and provides tangible proof of success to your employees. It's the evidence you'll need to prove that the effort met its objectives and delivered results. That's a good thing. But measuring at the end is only a way of assessing if your plan succeeded or failed. By that time, it's too late to do anything about it!

Thinking back to when we talked about creating objectives, we mentioned that you should attach measurable criteria to all of them. (In our example, we wanted the project team to identify the key goals and be able to articulate the initiative to others to 80 percent satisfaction.) In other words, we wanted to make sure that by the end of phase one, at least eight out of ten people had a clear understanding of our initiative. Of course, we wanted 100 percent satisfaction, but then again, we also wanted to be realistic about what we could feasibly accomplish in that period of time.

What Are the Ways to Measure?

Although there are many ways to measure, you want to think long and hard about what you're trying to accomplish, and then decide on the best format for checking your results. It's pretty obvious that you wouldn't want to use an e-survey if the people you are surveying don't have computers. However, there are other choices less obvious. Sometimes a focus group is not the best method because you have no tangible way to compile and analyze your data to come up with concrete results.

Here are some measurement techniques and tips on when you may want to use them:

- *Electronic surveys.* E-surveys are useful when you have several audiences and you need to survey them quickly and often as well as track trends. E-surveys can be used for both small surveys and larger ones, such as measuring employee attitudes companywide.
- *Hard-copy surveys.* These are similar to e-surveys; however, someone will have to compile the data into an electronic format so you can more easily work with it. These are good if you need to have hard documentation or if there is a lack of consistent computer access across your audiences.
- *Focus groups.* These are good for when you hit milestones in your project and you want rich, qualitative data from your audiences. They provide a good venue for soliciting lessons learned or for getting the pulse of your organization. Sometimes employees open up more when they're in a group. You don't always want to conduct electronic or written surveys because employees may begin to think they don't have a voice. They like it when you invite them to attend a focus group and share their opinions face to face alongside their

peers. Although it's important for your survey to be designed properly, you don't necessarily need anything as complex as a typical climate survey or a tool developed by Gallup. The important thing is that you be able to track movement in the results. By measuring focus groups at key intervals, you can see whether you're making progress. If you don't see positive change, it may be time to go back to the drawing board and revamp your communication plan.
- *Interviews.* In person or over the phone, one-on-one interviews are good for drawing out true feelings and being able to get the real lowdown. However, the participants would need to be reassured that their identities would be kept private (if that is their desire).
- *Informal feedback.* Everyone in a company can encourage this. Make sure your management keeps the lines of communication open to employees and constantly asks them how they're feeling and whether they have any feedback. Put a process in place for their feedback to be evaluated and actually be put to use. We don't just mean set up a suggestion box here. We mean talk to your employees. Let them see that they have an actual voice in your company and that you're doing what it takes to put their ideas into action.

Planning Tools for Measurement

We're planners. We admit it. When working on a large-scale internal marketing initiative, we needed some tools to make sure we could keep all our ducks in a row. We had a lot of audiences we were communicating with and we wanted to make sure we were measuring the effectiveness across the board. The templates, Figures 6.1 and 6.2, helped us to plan the ins and outs of our measurement scheme as well provide a visual for when we were going to do it.

FIGURE 6.1 Measurement Plan Logistics

Audience	Measurement Event	Vehicle	Date of Event	Results Compiled	Measurement Topics
Executives	Financial Communication Survey	Survey	8/18–8/22	8/29	1. Will they commit financially to initiative? 2. Do they feel costs are appropriate? 3. Do they understand need for confidentiality? 4. Do they have significant concerns?
Executives	Financial Communication Interviews	Key Exec Meeting and Interviews	8/18–9/19	9/26	Open-ended responses: 1. What are their concerns? 2. What additional communication is needed?
Directors/Managers	Budget Planning Survey	eSurvey/Quiz	9/1–9/5	9/12	1. How many have budgeted for initiative? 2. Do they understand how to budget appropriately?
Beta Testers	Post-July Summit Survey	eSurvey (link sent through e-mail and available at Kickoff Meeting)	7/21–7/25	8/1	1. Does staff understand the new changes? 2. How can we improve communication about changes for the next Beta group?
Beta Testers	Post-September Summit Survey	eSurvey	9/15	9/21	1. Does staff understand why we're doing this initiative? 2. Are they excited/bought into the initiative? 3. Do directors and managers know what to do to lead change? 4. How can we improve communication/training re: rollout?
Beta Testers	Beta Testing Lessons Learned Survey	eSurvey	1/12/2004–1/16/2004	1/23	1. What improvements should be made in communication and training for organizational rollout? 2. What other support should we provide to other directors/management when we do organizational rollout?
Beta Testers	Beta Testing Lessons Learned Interviews	Select Beta Testing BU Mgmt.	1/17–1/21 & 1/5/2004–1/9/2004	12/5 & 1/23	Open-ended responses: 1. Gather lessons learned from implementation. 2. What improvements should be made in communication and training for organizational rollout? 3. What other report should we provide to other management when we do organizational rollout?

A Match, a Zippo, or a Blowtorch | 139

FIGURE 6.2 Measurement Schedule

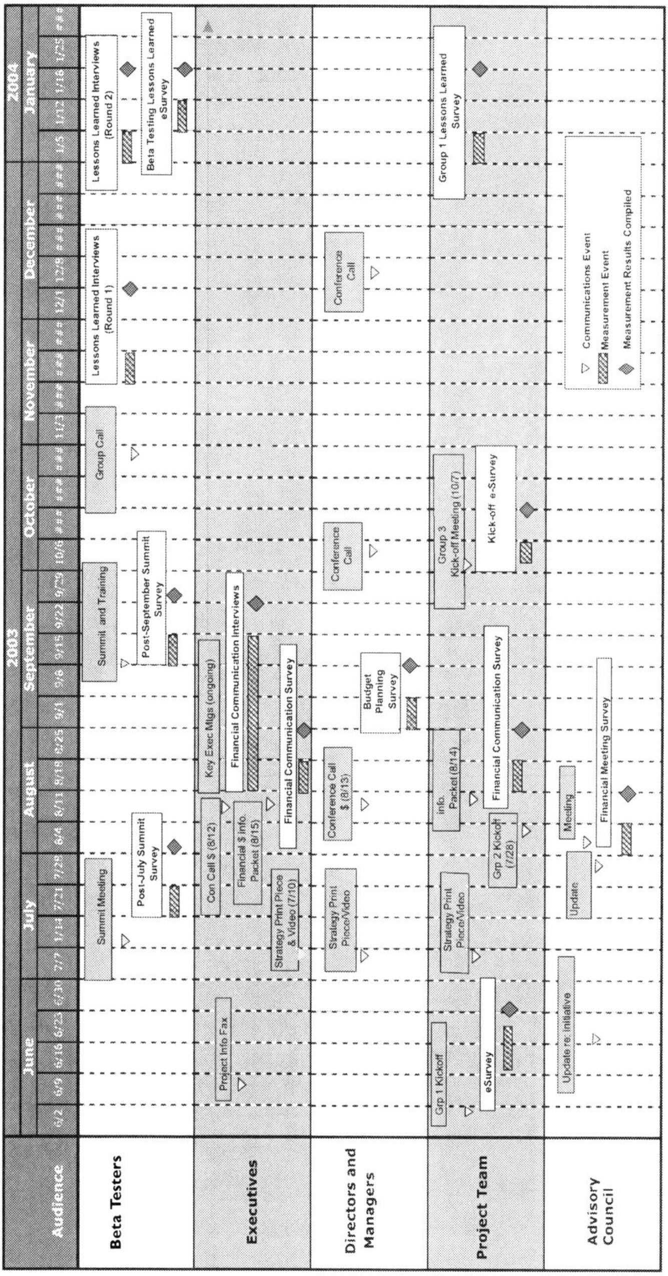

PRINCIPLES OF GOOD MARKETING

If you do only one thing to build a prosperous, successful brand, it should be this: Deliver on your brand promise—not once in a while, not most of the time, but *every* time. A brand is only as good as the promises to which it lives up. All the marketing in the world cannot save a brand that doesn't deliver on its promises (think Kmart and a few thousand dot-com companies).

Successful companies know better than to fail their customers, but there are still companies that fail their employees time and time again. Just as customers leave brands that fail them, so do employees.

The Need for Alignment

Words must match actions—period. If you can't make this one work, you may as well ditch your internal marketing mission.

I'm not sure which management book introduced us to the "walk the talk" theory, but that author gets a gold star. If every manager consistently walked the talk, we wouldn't be writing this book.

Sad to say, the disconnection of message and action is rampant in corporations today. Can't you just imagine the former Enron management team telling employees that they need to do a better job of submitting expense reports? Or the head of a dot-com asking employees to take their time and follow the rules?

This is not to say that mismatched message-action situations result from greed or lousy management. So few executives, managers, and supervisors understand how their actions are interpreted by people who don't walk in their shoes. And so often, employees twist or misinterpret managers' intentions.

We once did a project in which we ran a communications committee in the credit division of a major company. Initially, the group was comprised of about ten customer service employees.

At the outset, this group was exceptionally alienated from leadership. They felt a sense of entitlement and dissatisfaction. In fact, nothing management could do was right.

For the first few meetings, we allowed the employees to vent without interruption. We explored their feelings and let them get the hostility out of their systems. Then we started introducing the concept of "you can change it." The team began to take on projects that could enhance their work environment and make employees feel more appreciated. We talked about employees' feelings, and how employees perceived management.

The most interesting outcome of the situation is that when the team created activities designed for other employees, the employees did not resoundingly support the projects. In one instance of a departmental open house, people acted irresponsibly, signing up for duties they didn't carry out, griping about prizes not being good enough, and complaining that the team didn't do it right.

To say the communications committee members were upset is an understatement. They were livid at their coworkers. They finally understood how management felt. No speech or rule of operation could have changed the employees' perspective. Personal experience did.

Be Persistent and Consistent

Remember what we discussed in Chapter 3. Every industry has its mantra. For real estate, it's Location, Location, Location. In marketing, it's Repeat, Repeat, Repeat. Brands aren't born in a day. If you want to create awareness, enthusiasm, and buy-in of your internal brand, repeat the messages until people get them. And keep them consistent, because your brand will go nowhere if it's full of mixed signals. If you repeat the same messages over and over, you'll start creating an A+ brand.

Creating a brand takes time. In the case of a good advertising campaign, you can't live by the "quit while you're ahead" philosophy. To ingrain a theme in a customer's head takes many repetitions of message. By the time the ad team is utterly sick of a new creative approach, you can bet the customer is finally beginning to recognize it. Fortunately, there are usually some signs of progress even in the early stages of internal branding, but still we suggest you adopt one more quality, on top of being persistent and consistent—be patient too! It really does pay off.

Simple Sells

In our humble opinion, one of the geniuses of our time is Scott Adams, creator of the Dilbert cartoon strip that unveils a brand promise gone hopelessly awry. The pointy-haired boss talks and Dilbert hears blah, blah, blah. The boss is a Shakespearean player "that struts and frets his hour upon the stage and then is heard no more: it is a tale told by an idiot, full of sound and fury, signifying nothing."

Well, we can't shoot the messenger, so we have to teach him or her. The most important thing managers can know when it comes to communication is that they still sound smart even if they use simple words. I once read a capabilities brochure in which the bio of one of the principals talked about "visceral understanding." Please. Get rid of words that are not a part of everyday language. They will not make you sound more intelligent. They will make you sound out of touch with your audience.

And while you're at it, don't "ize" us to death. Lesson one in delivering your brand promise: Use English as a first language. Don't use jargon. Don't make up words. Don't use nouns as verbs or verbs as nouns. One last request: Look up the word *impacted* in the dictionary. It's not a verb meaning "to have an effect"; it's an adjective used to describe something like a tooth that is lodged in the body.

There's a simple test to measure readability. It's called the Gunning-Fog Index, and it tells you what grade level someone would have to have completed in order to understand the material. Most newspapers and magazines are written at about an eighth grade level. If you expect employees to understand your message, apply the Gunning-Fog Index to your last memo. Follow these five steps to determine the grade level of your communication:

1. Take a sample of the written communication that is about 100 words.
2. Divide the number of words by the number of sentences in the sample. This gives you the average number of words per sentence.
3. Count the number of words with three or more syllables.
4. Add the average number of words in a sentence and the number of words with three or more syllables.
5. Multiply the total by 0.4.

The final number represents the level of schooling a person must have completed to understand your writing. Thus, if the score was 5, someone in the fifth grade could understand it. If the score was 14, it means the reader would need 14 years of education to comprehend it. Here's an example of how to use this formula. Look at this writing sample:

> For example, if you developed a unique plant fertilizer that you manufacture and distribute, you should be able to establish that you created the fertilizer through extensive trial and error and then made sure that the employees learned the formula on a strict need-to-know basis.
> Similarly, if you put together a valuable customer list that includes your customers' buying history and buying habits, you should be able to show that you painstakingly built up the list over several years and that you only allowed a limited number of employees to see it.

This sample includes 92 words. Divide 92 by the number of sentences (2) for an average of 46 words per sentence. We count

19 words of three or more syllables. Now we add the average words per sentence (42) to the number words of three or more syllables (19). Our total is 61. Finally, we multiply 61 times 0.4. The score for this sample is 24, meaning that the average person would need 24 years of school to understand it.

Now try testing a sample of your writing, such as the latest e-mail you sent to someone in your company. What was the score? If it was above 12, you're losing readership. Simplify and you'll enjoy higher readership levels and higher understanding—both essentials of a good internal marketing plan.

Is There Such a Thing as Too Much Communication?

The average person in America is bombarded with tens of thousands of ideas every day—from family letters and calls to advertising messages, political sound bites, the TV news, and their own company's e-mail system. Realistically, people can only process a finite number of ideas at one time. The rest are filtered out. If your internal marketing campaign tries to incorporate too many different ideas, your employees are going to filter them out as well. Simplicity is the key. In the beginning, give your employees only one or two key messages to absorb.

The biggest mistake we see in most companies' communications is overcommunication. When we say that, we mean that companies send employees *too many messages* and tell them *too many extraneous things.* They can't possibly sift through all the unnecessary words to figure out what you're trying to say. Get to the point. Let's say you are a shoe manufacturer and you release the following corporate communication to your employees:

> Our shoes are made in Greenland with 72.3 percent rubber, 16.7 percent high-grade canvas, 3 percent Corinthian leather, .6 percent silicone gel, .4 percent oxyliquipermutol, and 7 percent air. We ship them to markets in 59 countries, 12 provinces, and 82 emirates, identifying out-

lets that have both young and adult customers. Our market mix is 50 percent males between 10 and 23 years old who live in suburbs in the Northern hemisphere of fewer than 34,567 residents.

Now throw in a few "ize" words:

Our goal is to prioritize markets so we can maximize our sales and optimize our profits, thereby utilizing our employees' ideas.

Congratulations. You have reached critical mass with ineffective communication.

Who cares about all that stuff you just said? Most of that information is completely useless to the average employee. And while you may think this exercise is silly, we've seen countless e-mails, newsletters, presentations, and other media with this type of overkill. This type of communication is like pouring soup on a campfire. You end up with a lot of smoke and no one can eat the soup.

There's a reason ads are comprised of a few carefully selected short words. It works.

In your own communications, get to the point: We make good shoes. People like them. This is how you contribute to it. Just do it. Thank goodness there are companies such as Nike that understand this.

Just One Thing

A number of years ago, comedian Billy Crystal starred in the movie *City Slickers* about three city boys who go on vacation to a working ranch. Billy's character, in the midst of a midlife crisis, is searching for the meaning of life. He approaches Jack Palance, who plays the trail boss, and asks him to share his wisdom. Palance replies, "There's just one thing." Crystal tries throughout the movie to find out what that "one thing" is. Unfortunately, the trail boss dies before he can find out.

You're luckier than Billy. You know what your "one thing" is. It's your company's brand promise. State it clearly. Repeat it often. And by all means, keep it simple.

Is Everyone Pulling in the Same Direction?

It's a little more complicated than rubbing two sticks together, but now you know most of the steps to take to work up a nice-sized bonfire in your company. A word of advice: The process isn't something you'll do perfectly the first time around. In fact, we're not sure anyone can ever do it perfectly. Life just isn't so cut and dried. Rest easy, though. When you make an attempt to follow these guidelines, we predict you'll be 100 percent closer to having fired-up employees than you've ever been before.

Once the oars are in the water, you can keep everyone pulling in the same direction by recognizing their efforts. That's the topic of Chapter 9, recognition and rewards.

Respect people. Tell the truth. Honor employees' efforts to carry out your brand promise. That's the way you light their fire. And we wouldn't be surprised if the results light your fire, too!

Chapter 7

TRAINING AS A MARKETING TOOL

"All we really have as a company is our people's skills or the fruit of their skills," says Mike Hill, general manager of the Telecommunications Group at IBM. "It's in a company's best interest to guarantee that their people's skills are as updated as possible." Companies that don't take a serious interest in employee training and development can't sell them or keep them.

Training increases employees' skills and ensures they have the knowledge necessary to do their jobs well. That's a given. But have you ever considered what it could mean to use training as a marketing tool?

Not only can training heighten employee morale and commitment, but it also can orient and get everyone on the same page in respect to your company's visions and goals. An investment in training shows employees that you care about them and want to invest in their growth. In times of change, it can decrease their anxiety and lead them to accept and buy in to new roles and expectations. When you combine communication with training you *enable* your employees to deliver your brand promise to customers.

HOW CAN COMPANIES USE TRAINING AS A MARKETING TOOL?

These are a few ways that training can be used as a marketing tool:

- To grow, develop, and satisfy employees
- To get employees on the same page and speaking with one voice
- To gain employees' buy-in for change

GROW, DEVELOP, AND SATISFY EMPLOYEES

President Dwight D. Eisenhower said, "Pull the string, and it will follow wherever you wish. Push it, and it will go nowhere at all." It's a fitting description of how to get employees to carry out your mission—inspire performance rather than mandate it. Training assists in that process.

Phyllis Huang, a training manager at Gap Inc. (Gap, Banana Republic, and Old Navy brands) believes employee training has a dual marketing benefit:

1. It shows employees that their company is dedicated to their development and growth.
2. It demonstrates to potential employees and other companies that it is a great place to work and do business.

Phyllis had heard about Gap Inc.'s "best in class" employee training and development program prior to her employment there, and ultimately it was a big determining factor in her choice to work there.

What's In It for Me?

Why is training important to Phyllis Huang, Gap Inc. employee? First, it adds competencies to her resume free of charge. Second, it shows her that her company appreciates her hard work, wants her to succeed, and is willing to invest in her future.

It's no wonder that Phyllis loves Gap Inc., and praises it to anyone and everyone who will listen. She sees her company as one that is investing in her and providing her with marketable skills. She has told me numerous times that this is what makes her want to stay with the company long term. A company that demonstrates its investment in employees exhibits to employees that it is committed to their success.

Singapore Airlines is known as a top employer. One of the primary reasons is that the SIA Group invests over $100 million on training each year, far exceeding Singapore's national average per worker. Imagine this: Its investment in employee training forms the largest component of the airline's operating expenditure, clearly illustrating the link it sees between staff development and profitability. That's not the size of the training budget you usually find even in huge companies.

Through training, you're showing your employees that you expect a high-performing organization. You're sending a message by providing them with top-notch skills and knowledge of which they can be proud. By giving employees professional skills training, you ensure their effectiveness on the job, and tap into their personal growth and development as well.

But training's not just about how much more work you can get out of people. Let employees take fun classes to learn how to make pottery, buy a house, appreciate music, or perhaps something important yet not as fun, such as tax planning. It's easy to get experts outside of your company to come in and conduct these classes for little or no charge. And employees will be energized by the change of pace from the regular workday!

If you use training and succession planning tools, employees can see that you want them to stick around and that you're committed to promoting from within. Many companies lose the trust of their employees over time by not incorporating a real plan for growth and promotion. Employees feel as if they're just warm bodies slaving away thanklessly. It's hard to have emotional loyalty toward your employer if you don't feel it has any concern for your welfare.

Adult learners are motivated when they control their own destiny and growth, so get your employees involved in their own development and career pathing. Let them tell you what types of training they want and need. Give them a variety of curriculum options to choose from and empower them to take charge of their own development plan.

Whether you're providing professional or personal development training, it must be deemed valuable by your employees. Employees want solid, practical training they can apply. By the same token, they're reluctant to waste their time on training if they believe it will be too academic or provide them with no immediate value. When they see the connection to how they can apply their learning immediately to their jobs, or for enjoyment and growth in other areas of their lives, they embrace training with enthusiasm and appreciation.

Employees may want or need to attend training but can't pull away from their responsibilities to pursue it. Provide employees with the time to train. Clear their schedules so they don't feel punished by coming back to a huge stack of work. Better yet, have others take on their role for that period of time so the training isn't "just one more thing" they have to pile on top of the rest of their work.

At the end of the day, employees will be inspired to support goals. When people are ordered to do something, they may do it, but they'll do it without enthusiasm. When people are inspired to do something, they do so with enthusiasm, dedication, and joy.

Cross-Training and Test-Driving New Roles

To people who enjoy a good challenge, there's nothing more boring than the same old same old. Often, employees leave their companies because they're in a rut, frustrated with performing the same responsibilities over and over, day after day.

Want to be a great company? Develop structured career planning programs that include cross-training on functional skills, job rotations, and project management assignments that are of interest to a wide range of employees. Give employees a chance to learn new technologies and methods. Capture long-term interest from high-potential performers by letting them try out new roles and take on tougher assignments. They'll gain exposure while building self-esteem and credibility that's valuable for them and the company.

Over time, you'll find that opportunity and recognition can prove to be a much more lucrative incentive than any financial considerations you might offer.

Missed Opportunities

In one of the companies I worked for previously, management was creating new positions in the area of consulting in which I was interested—change management. The minute these jobs were posted internally, I excitedly called our vice president. "Brad!" I gushed. "I saw these positions posted and this is exactly the type of work that I would love to do!" I proceeded to ask him what I could do to get one of these jobs. He flatly replied, "Well, Sara, we're going to hire from a Big Five firm for these positions."

Oh, I see. A Big Five firm. It took me a minute to swallow that news. But I was undaunted. "Well, Brad, is there anything I can do to job-shadow, be mentored, or get on a development path to move into one of these positions eventually?"

He replied that perhaps I could talk to someone who was already in one of these roles to get more information. You see, there wasn't really a formal plan they could offer to help me develop into that role.

I was disheartened and sad that I had given so much loyalty, hard work, and long hours to a company that seemed to cast my desires aside that quickly. My performance reviews were stellar, but I was becoming bored in my current role. I wasn't feeling challenged anymore. Hadn't they been the ones, in my initial interview, who asked me where I wanted to be in five years? I had told them my aspirations, but clearly they had no intention of helping me reach them.

I decided that if they weren't invested in my development, I'd leave. I promptly gave my company notice and joined—you guessed it—a Big Five firm.

Perhaps some of your employees aren't well suited for their particular positions but would flourish in other roles. Consider establishing a mini internship program, in which employees shadow coworkers or their managers for a day to learn more about their roles and responsibilities. This test-drive might spark new ideas about increased value from the employee, and allow you to see where a role-shift may make sense for the company. Even if it doesn't result in changing roles, employees relish being more well-rounded and feeling they have a broad wealth of skills.

At Southwest Airlines, they have the Walk a Mile program, in which any employee can do somebody else's job for a day. Naturally, the operations agents cannot fly the planes—Southwest isn't that freewheeling—but the pilots can, and do, work as operations agents. (They also, on their own, have held barbecues for all the mechanics, to thank them for keeping the planes flying.) Seventy-five percent of Southwest's 20,000 employees have participated in the job-swapping program. "It's an administrative nightmare, but one of the best tools I know for building understanding and collaboration," says Herb Kelleher. Hear that? An administrative nightmare. How many companies do you know that would have stopped right there?

Coaching

Another reason that employees suffer from low morale is they feel as though they're not getting necessary feedback and coaching to grow. When you coach employees, you can inspire personal satisfaction on the job. It's amazing how a person can elevate her commitment to excellence. And here's where you can foster the person's development as a leader, if that's her ultimate goal.

Good coaching requires that you let employees know promptly how they are doing and provide a lot of helpful feedback:

- Adapt your approach to each individual.
- Recognize and reward success.
- Most important, tell employees immediately when they've done a job well. It's the critical element to their overall happiness.

Direct feedback on a job well done is especially helpful to an employee. Give specific feedback such as, "I wanted to tell you that your attention to detail on that quality report was amazing." This tells the employee exactly what they're doing well and encourages them to repeat that desired behavior time and time again.

IBM is known for its attention to training, and its coaching program helps employees learn what they need to know to move up. Mike Hill is one of the executives involved.

"I'm a formal mentor to 12 people, and I also have an 'early identified' sales rep," he says. "I was told to identify someone in my organization who has real talent. I act as an independent coach to her on career decisions. She'll come in and sit in on my meetings; she can discuss things outside her chain."

Mike explains that every level of management is involved and every single executive participates. Before you get promoted, "one of the leadership traits we look for is coaching," says Mike. "You can't get promoted without having been a successful coach."

He explains that he, too, has a mentor. Employees at all levels can select a person they admire to be a mentor. "I almost picked [an executive], but I knew he was next in line to be CEO, and he wouldn't have time for me after he gets promoted," he laughs.

"At my level, there are executive coaches from Human Resources I can contact to improve my leadership and diagnostic skills. They sit in on my meetings to observe. One of my coaches is working with us on a communications plan to our employees about how we become a real leadership group on our growth initiatives. We're looking at which media to use and what messages we need to communicate to get employees into a different mindset about risk and growth."

Mentoring

Mentoring is typically done within a more formal structure than coaching. It's put into place in many companies as an additional strategy for employee development. Mentoring brings two people together to achieve specific objectives for the protégé's growth and skills. A good mentoring program connects the experienced and the less experienced so that "business smarts" and knowledge can be passed on. These types of partnerships are usually monitored and tracked.

Some best practices for growing and developing employees are:

- Understand each employee's strengths and needs.
- Challenge them with opportunities for development.
- Foster innovation by allowing room for failure.
- Ask for and act on employee feedback and ideas.
- Provide opportunities to train in other company functions.
- Coach for success.
- Set up formal mentoring programs.

GETTING EVERYONE ON THE SAME PAGE

Orientation: The Message Starts Here

Employees will never be more excited than the first day they're hired. Take advantage of their positive outlook to get them fired up about your vision. Your recruiting and hiring practices give employees a glimpse of your corporate culture, but orientation is the first formal opportunity you have to begin to ingrain your philosophy in employees.

Does your orientation look like this?

- Employees arrive and are given a stick-on "Hello My Name Is . . ." badge and a package with a hodgepodge of materials. These include bad copies of indecipherable benefits information, 12 forms to fill out, directions to get a parking pass, an out-of-date map of the facility and a smiley face sticker.
- The head of Human Resources welcomes people and shows a talking head video of the CEO saying how important employees are.
- A stream of department representatives parades in and out to tell about their areas. Some are on time, some late, and some are fill-ins who don't know the material very well. Of the six who present, one is a skilled speaker who makes the information interesting.
- At noon they have lunch in the employee cafeteria.
- During the afternoon they visit their departments to find out where the bathrooms are, where their cubicle is located, how to sign themselves up for a phone, and where the supply cabinet is.

If this is truly what your orientation looks like, we can almost guarantee that employees aren't feeling exuberant about their new jobs. One of our clients, a CEO, was enraged when he spoke to a group of new employees and one, sitting directly in front of him, fell asleep.

So, beyond "Here's when you get a paycheck, here's how we fill out expense reports . . . " make this a time to build employees' pride in your organization. Share your history, culture, and vision—what your company is all about and how the new employee fits into that scheme. Never discount the importance of embedding these messages into your training. Orientation is the time to get new hires on board mentally and emotionally. It's your chance to gain buy-in and start building loyalty. New employees want to believe they've joined a special place. Tell them, "Here's the value you bring to us, and here's the value we bring to you." Show them how their role will further the company's growth and how it's a mutually advantageous relationship. Involve executives. When the top dogs participate, it tells new employees: You're important to us and we're honored you came to work here.

Levi Strauss and Company, based in San Francisco, is a company with strong values and history. It emphasizes social responsibility in its new-hire orientation. Its main objective is to introduce employees to what the company stands for, and to enable employees to feel part of that stronger purpose. It also strives to show them their role in that quest.

The orientation is comprised of stories about the company's past and what it did in the quest for equality and social responsibility. Each part of the orientation strives to integrate brand values and social responsibilities and their effect on the business over the years. One example describes how Levi Strauss halted a manufacturing plant in the practice of segregating black and white workers in the 1960s.

The current trend in new employee orientation is to follow these three steps:

1. Introduce employees to the business culture and identity.
2. Define how their specific work as, say, a finance person or a manufacturing person translates or relates to the other areas of the company.

3. Show how their role contributes to the company's overall success. When orientation describes the company's vision and goals, what an individual does in his position, and how that links to business results, everyone is getting the same message and starts off on the same page.

Our friend, Phyllis Huang, is one of the training managers responsible for rethinking and developing the new-hire orientation at Gap Inc. They have dubbed their new-hire process the "strategy cascade," because it goes from big picture to smaller picture. It covers overall company new-hire orientation all the way down to each employee's functional area and specific role within the company.

Here's how Gap Inc.'s orientation process works:

- *Gap Inc. organizationwide orientation.* This is for everyone in the company. The strategy gets set here. In the subsequent new-hire courses, an employee can see how the strategy is affected every step of the way.
- *Brand orientation.* This is specific to the brands within Gap Inc. The employee would go to the appropriate orientation based on whether they worked for the Gap, Banana Republic, or Old Navy brand.
- *Executive orientation.* This is the next step for executives after they have completed the organizational and brand orientations. This is leadership training that combines all brand executives to ensure a cohesive vision across Gap Inc.
- *Functional orientation.* This is specific to each employee's function (such as Banana Republic planning, Gap merchandising, Old Navy design), and its role in the overall success of the organization.
- *Role orientation.* The final step of the new-hire orientation is to attend training for the role. For example, managers and directors within a merchandising function would attend the merchandising manager orientation. An individual contributor would attend the merchandising analyst orientation.

Following orientation, employees are eligible to attend development classes. In these classes, employees design an action plan for how they will meet business goals in their new role. They align action plans with the business function goals. (An example of a goal could be to send designs for Fall 2005 apparel to production by X date). The action plan would include a statement of the strategy, objectives, deliverables, and any interdependencies the employee may have.

Once the employees are satisfied with their plans, they share the plans with their managers. The managers help employees shape their plans and then are responsible for holding employees accountable for implementation. Remember what we said before: An employee feels more valued and trusted when he has the autonomy to create a plan for how he believes he and his function can succeed.

Gap Inc. is carefully constructing its employment planning to ensure orientation links to employee development and development links to succession planning. Within the course of an employee's development path, the employee, if she wishes, can rotate to do her same job within another one of the company's brands. She is also able to participate in cross-functional job rotation.

As far as curriculum goes, employees have many choices within their development path. Employees select the courses and activities they believe would be best for their development and present their recommendations to their managers on how that would specifically add value to their job and organization.

From an internal marketing perspective, this is an ideal world—one in which the company's goals and employees' goals are forever intertwined.

Skills Training and Company Philosophy Equal a Happy Union

Smart companies hire for attitude and train for skills. Thus, it's more important to hire someone with the right personality, attitude, and values than all the right experience. Of course, that also means you're going to have to provide skills training. But at the end of the day, if you've hired people with the right attitudes and aptitude, and trained them for skills, you're bound to be more successful and have better results retaining employees as well.

Many organizations use the skills training process to embed the brand's values. It's important that the training process focus on programs that are defined by the company's values. For example, if creativity is a core value of the company then that skill has to be nurtured.

To get people to realize their creativity, unleash them from the rational constraints of their day-to-day jobs. Here's a situation that illustrates what we mean. It starts with a tree house.

At a large telecommunications company management challenged us to use creative techniques to teach engineers how to use new processes for technical development. The engineers' training was to be centered on the creation of two new technical processes, using the new design documents for their technical projects. We knew we would have to employ creative tactics; otherwise, the engineers would get bogged down in the details of specifications. We wanted them to think in an entirely new way.

We designed a simulation in which they used the documents they would typically use to build a network plan to create a tree house. Picture this: a bunch of engineers, building tree houses out of cardboard, and decorating them with fake foliage from Hobby Lobby. They were skeptical, but at the end of our six-hour training, they told us working with an example far from their traditional "product line" helped them to think creatively and learn the process without the constraints of their everyday thinking.

Southwest Airlines also ensures its core values are integrated into its training. According to Fritz Petree, senior manager of career development services and Virtual University at Southwest Airlines' University for People, close cooperation between the company and its employees leads to a customer focus based on the Golden Rule.

"It's a major cultural focus to just do the right thing, regardless of rules, regardless of things that are put in place," he explained. "We select courses that are customer-focused rather than process- or business-focused. So we focus on the employee first in the company to make sure they're fulfilled and have the opportunities to learn and grow. We think, in turn, they will treat customers the same way. By empowering employees to do the right thing, Southwest ensures high-quality customer service and drives up productivity. We encourage altruism, teamwork, and shared effort in employees."

Train as Though Every Employee Is a Corporate Representative

If employees identify with their company, they are more inclined to be loyal to it. Train employees to succinctly articulate your brand's vision and promise, and to understand how they carry out that vision. Imagine that every single one of your employees is your corporate spokesperson. They need to be polished and knowledgeable when they speak to others about your company's services and products. Just as you would use media training to enable your corporate spokesperson to stay on message, increase shareholder confidence, or announce new product or service lines, you can use your training to incorporate messages and knowledge for all your employees.

In summary, here are some best practices for getting employees on the same page:

- Use orientation as a way to get employees speaking with one voice.
- Use skills training to embed your company philosophy and values.
- Use training as if every employee is your corporate spokesperson.

THE CHANGE EXPERIENCE: GAINING THEIR BUY-IN

Nearly every person in the working world has experienced a reorganization, merger, downsizing, upsizing, backsliding, or a cross-function or a business transformation of one type or another. Any way you slice it, it's scary and disorienting. Where employees are concerned, you can't exactly send them to therapy to help them overcome their fears. But you can use training to support employees when they're feeling anxious about changes within your company.

Once employees feel secure that they still have their jobs, they will begin to worry about how their work may be changing. Rest assured that your team will be unsettled for some period of time no matter what assurance you give. As things settle down, you can provide training to demonstrate to your employees that you are invested in their success.

I've been part of many enterprisewide systems implementations that would have been more readily accepted if employees had known they'd be supported and would be trained to help them succeed in their new roles and work. Tell employees far in advance that they will have all the tools and training to help them when the changes come. Include information gradually, throughout communications, instead of springing things on them as an afterthought. Offer succinct communications to them about what training will be and what it will not be. In your marketing communications about the training, you can tout the fact that you're providing employees with world-class skills that will make them very marketable (just in case).

Training can also build credibility for a new method you are thinking about using in your company. For example, say you're considering implementing an entirely new sales process or you're changing your company's selling methods to emphasize value and relationship. You can use training in this new sales process to enable employees to understand the new procedures and help you to gain their buy-in and support before you even switch to the new method. The training should answer the question "Why should I change how I've been selling?" Elements of good learning include an awareness that you have to change, acceptance of the fact, commitment to the need to change, and most important, teaching the right skills to get to the right outcome.

Here are a couple best practices for using training to gain employees' buy-in for change:

1. Offer comprehensive change communications and training to show employees that you will provide them with all the tools and skills necessary for success in the new environment.
2. Use training as a way to get buy-in and understanding for changes you may make in the future.

SOME OTHER THINGS TO KEEP IN MIND

Just as it's important to measure whether our communication is effective, we also need a way to determine if our training works. Why would we waste our dollars and time on something we weren't sure worked? It seems a silly question but you'd be surprised how many companies write off training as just something they needed to do before they could move to the next step. They consider that once training is complete, "the people part" is done. They never really measure to see if the training paid off or helped change behavior.

Here are some things you want to measure after training:

- From a marketing or employee satisfaction angle, you want to know if the training made a difference in the way employees feel about their readiness, motivation, and enthusiasm.
- Regarding skills and knowledge, you want to know if the training made a tangible difference once employees put those abilities to work when they're back at the job.

There are many things to look for in your measurement and you'll have to determine exactly what information you're trying to derive.

Evaluate Your Training for Effectiveness

For many years, Donald Kirkpatrick's four levels of evaluation have been used to determine training effectiveness within corporations.

Level 1 (evaluating reaction). Immediately after training, the employees give their feedback. If you've ever taken training, you've probably received a "smiley face" sheet at the end of class that asks you what you thought about the instructor, the content, and so on.

When creating and using a Level 1 or "training reaction" evaluation, consider these guidelines:

- Determine what you want to find out and measure.
- Design an evaluation that quantifies reactions. In other words, one that uses numbers that are trackable over time.
- Encourage written comments and suggestions to get true, honest input in the words of your participants.
- Make sure you convey the importance of the evaluation to the participant. In other words, you'll be using the evaluations to make sure that training is effectively meeting their needs.
- Introduce the evaluation form at the beginning of class, so participants may fill it in throughout the course. You'll want them to react as they're experiencing it. Besides, most will bolt right at the end!
- Determine what evaluation results are acceptable standards.
- Compare reactions to the standards, then determine how this will be reported and communicated.

Level 2 (evaluating learning). During training, employees will demonstrate their pretraining and posttraining skills through a test or skills check.

When creating and using a Level 2 or "learning" evaluation, consider these guidelines:

- Determine what you want to measure. What knowledge or skills do you want developed or improved? What attitudes were changed?
- Map back to course objectives. Design an evaluation that tests the mastery of specific skills or attitudes as identified by course objectives.
- If you're teaching concepts, principles, and techniques that may already be known, evaluate knowledge, skills, and attitudes *before* and *after* the program.
- Make it fun! Create a game to measure skills and knowledge.
- Use paper and pen for more formal testing; use polling questions for informal evaluations.
- Use the results of the evaluation to modify the learning process, materials, or environment.

Level 3 (evaluating behavior). Usually 45 to 90 days after training has taken place, a Level 3 evaluation (whether a survey or actual on-the-job observation) will take place to see if employees were able to apply their new skills and attitudes in their jobs. This evaluation identifies if one of the following three conclusions were made:

1. "I like what happened and plan to use the new behavior."
2. "I don't like what happened and will go back to my old behavior."
3. "I like what happened but the boss or other restraints prevent me from doing it."

When creating and using a Level 3 or "behavior" evaluation, consider these guidelines:

- Determine what you want to measure. Which skills or attitudes do you want to observe?
- Map your evaluation back to course objectives!
- Identify skills or knowledge that were once used but are no longer used, and why use was stopped.
- Allow time for the behavior to take place before doing such an evaluation.
- Survey or interview one or more of the following: The employee, his supervisor, his subordinates, and others who often observe his behavior.
- Determine how the results will be reported and communicated.

Level 4 (evaluating results and impact). The objective of the Level 4 evaluation is to describe the expected outcome and performance that should be influenced by the training. This could focus on things such as output, quality, costs, time, customer service skills, or inspired work climate.

When creating and using a Level 4 or "results" evaluation, consider these guidelines:

- You must gather "hard data" in categories such as productivity, cost control, and profitability to measure the impact training had on those areas.
- You also need "soft data," such as employees' levels of motivation and satisfaction, and their general attitude. You can figure this out through past employee satisfaction surveys, employee turnover, and work habits such as absenteeism and tardiness. Soft data is not easy to compile, so you should seek the assistance of an expert in data collection and analysis to help you to isolate the effects of the training program and determine what impact, if any, it had on those areas.

- Make sure you have a plan for how you will communicate results as well as an action plan for using them.

Use Experiential Learning

> "What I hear, I forget. What I see, I remember.
> What I do, I understand."
> **CONFUCIUS, 450 BC**

Put simply, experiential learning is learning by doing. This means that during training students apply their new skills "hands on" through role-playing, case studies, or other active methods. This sure beats being lectured to. This type of learning motivates students and empowers them to take control of their own learning. Upon leaving training, students feel more prepared and confident to immediately apply their new skills back to the job because they've had a chance to practice in a no-risk environment.

Market Your Training Internally and Externally

Here are some guidelines for marketing your training:

- Market your training to appropriate audiences with enough frequency to build interest.
- Show them the value of attending. If the company allocates time, employees will be more relaxed to attend. It's not much fun to go to training and fall behind in your work.
- Ensure that training is a management priority for everyone and not a punishment for people who attend.

It's no mistake that the most revered and successful companies in the business world happen to be ones that offer their employees the most opportunities for training and career development. Companies often use their employee training and development plan to show the outside world that they care about and grow their employees. They're sending the message to those potential customers that their employees will deliver better products and services as a result. It can also be a marketing tool to show potential employees that your company is a great place to work. When evaluating job offers, potential employees rank training and career development opportunities as one of the most important factors. Before taking positions, many of the skilled and desirable candidates ask what types of formal and on-the-job training they will receive, what types of coaching and mentoring they can expect, and what career growth opportunities are available. These candidates want to know that if they come to your company, they will have all the tools necessary to help them be successful.

Build a Social Network for Your Employees through Training

Our employees face a world of information overload, rapid change, and uncertainty. On top of that, they're working in an organization where they need new knowledge and skills constantly to keep up. As a result of all of this, they can become very anxious and defensive.

One of the ways that employees feel safer in taking these steps is to be connected to other people and feel they are included in a group. In other words, they can take solace in the fact that they are not alone. When they are learning with others, they have the emotional and intellectual support that allows them to go beyond, to feel more comfortable with their ever-changing set of circumstances.

Place participants in teams and give them tasks in which they depend upon each other to complete the learning. You'll find this technique meets their inherent social needs. They tend to be more engaged and afterward will have a network of peers. When employees have a "community of practice" they are happier with their jobs, more connected with their companies, and feel more supported in their roles.

Give them a support network and a chance to work together, as a team, to solve business problems. On this topic, Herb Kelleher of Southwest Airlines says, "Training is another way you forge committed partnership. Naturally, an airline must train every employee, but our most important training is not in how to manage or administer but in how to lead. Originally that training was part of our pilots' crew-resource management program. It focused on how the first officer and the pilot relate to each other, how they exchange information, and how they focus on the task at hand. In short, how they work as a team. Today we have reservation sales agents, flight attendants, mechanics, administrative staff in those classes, as well as the cockpit crews."

Use Employees as Trainers

Consultants may not be the perfect trainers because employees may think, "Hey, they don't know our business." So rather than just running out to grab consultants or outsourcing services for training every time, consider using employees as trainers. They can bring credibility and knowledge to your training because they are industry subject matter experts and have company know-how.

The one catch to using employee trainers is that you must make sure they're prepared to deliver effective training. Knowing how to deliver training isn't something that's intuitive. It takes someone who knows how to transfer what they know to others in a very tangible and clear manner. It also takes patience and working well with others. Get some of your biggest brand champions and train them to be trainers. It shows the rest of your employees that their colleagues are bought in and helps to cement training integrity.

Make Training Fun!

Put variety in your training to wow your employees! Consider alternatives to lecturing. Get your employees out on field trips, play a game to test their skills and knowledge, use fun role-playing scenarios—anything to just have fun while they learn.

The Boston Beer Company conducts training that is both experiential and an all-around good time for employees. Instead of just hearing about the brewing method, employees experience it firsthand! They learn about the brewing method, the ingredients, the history, and then, they create their own beer! Employees love it when they receive their beer in the mail 21 days later—right after the brewing process is complete.

No matter how you do it, make sure you don't miss out on the opportunity to show your employees that they can have a little fun at work, especially in learning.

Chapter

8

D2D

The Sum Is Greater than the Parts

You've heard the term B2B, meaning business to business. I have my own term for a different type of internal marketing—D2D, department to department.

When I say this out loud I'm always reminded of R2-D2 from *Star Wars*. And, of course, what's R2-D2 without C-3PO? You'll recall that R2-D2 is a spunky, loyal droid, and C-3PO is a by-the-book droid who knows hundreds of languages. Together, their diehard loyalty and communication skills make them a powerful team.

The same is true when departments within a company work together harmoniously; the strengths of one complement the strengths of the other.

Yet often departments work in an insular climate, unaware of each other's activities, oblivious about their resources, alienated by territorial disputes, isolated by distance or by function, or, worst of all, saboteurs of each other because of differences in priorities or clashing personalities. You'd think we were describing the Hatfields and McCoys.

On the other hand, there are corporate departments such as human resources or IT that by their very nature touch all areas of the company. Even though they're more visible than most, these groups don't always get their fair share of accolades. Though their work may be outstanding, they may not be respected for the contributions they make. Why? In some cases, it's because they work behind the scenes, and frequently neither employees nor associates know or value what they do.

At the highest levels, departments may be in sync; senior executives understand the links and shared strategic goals. But as you move farther down the organization, closer to the tactical decisions, line-level actions, and, most important, to customers, this understanding breaks down and support declines.

When departments don't work well together, their output suffers. Systems fail. Training misses the mark. Products have engineering flaws. Deliveries are off schedule. And voilà! The customer is unhappy. Everything that happens everywhere in the company affects customers—for better or for worse.

CINDERELLA FINDS HER GLASS SLIPPER

Here's a Cinderella story I experienced. When I joined Holiday Inns, Inc., 25 years ago as a staff writer, our department was undersized and underloved. Management had little, if any, regard for what we did. We were not a profit center; therefore, we simply drained the corporate coffers. When the time came for budget cuts, we were the ones under the knife. We were the quintessential char girl, left to do chores and clean up messes.

About a year after I joined the company, we got a new corporate communications director, Jerry Daly, a hotshot with PR experience at giants like Burson-Marsteller. Burson-Marsteller was a true powerhouse, especially in the crisis management arena. In 1982, when seven people died from poisoned Tylenol, it helped

Johnson & Johnson respond to the public with honesty and integrity.

Coming from that kind of background, Jerry was a heavy hitter who put our department in a tailspin with his wild and crazy ideas. Most of us in the department had a very limited concept of our role in the company, and virtually no thoughts about the valuable contribution our department could make to the corporation. In fact, the longest-term vision I could muster was in regard to my own career: I was editor of our weekly newsletter, and I aspired to eventually become the editor of the monthly magazine. As someone who needed a steady job, status quo was okay with me; I never dreamed of rocking the boat.

But not Jerry. His idea was to make us a valued resource to other departments and a respected member of the management team. When we listened to what he was saying, you'd have thought he had asked us, "Hey, how about we take all the information in the whole world and put it on a network where everyone can use it and plug it into something called a computer?" In 1979, his idea was just as unimaginable.

But Jerry had a way of helping us see his vision. His enthusiasm was contagious. We began by interviewing the key people in human resources, marketing, operations, development, and so on, to find out their area's most pressing issues, not so much related to communication as to their business unit goals. The listening sessions gave us the information we needed plus a chance to introduce everyone to our new client-driven approach. Our presentations were heavily laced with money-saving ideas because that was a quick way to their hearts. Once we had their attention, we were able to show them how we could contribute to their ability to succeed. The managers began to see us as partners who could contribute to their efforts.

Three of us and an assistant covered the key departments, cranking out projects fast and furious. All the while, Jerry was making presentations to senior management, citing our success stories. He had me compile a quarterly report of projects that demonstrated how much money we had saved by using our internal resources versus outside PR or ad agencies. Within a year, by Jerry's calculations, we had saved the company about $500,000. And we had made our team proud.

In the midst of the hard work we were doing, Jerry made sure there was fun. He believed in supporting the community, so he picked an annual fund-raising 5K race and signed us all up. Our department at that time consisted of about 33 women and two men. He made the race a men-against-women challenge, and he called it (unofficially) the First Annual Sexist Race. Not exactly politically correct, but we took it in the spirit it was intended. It accomplished exactly what Jerry was hoping it would. It was fun and boosted our morale and team spirit.

Over the next two years, our department achieved new stature in the company. Our vice president now reported directly to the CEO. We won Gold Quill and Silver Anvil awards from the two top business communications associations. Our staff had grown to 35 professionals and we had an annual budget of about $3 million. In that day, it was a phenomenal number.

That story was the 1980 version of D2D, which at the time was revolutionary. Jerry virtually single-handedly revamped our department using his own energy and vision, dragging along a young, naïve group of people who discovered they could change their destiny. It is a wonderful example of how even one person with a burning desire can transform a department's reputation and its credibility.

BRANDING BEFORE BRANDING WAS COOL

One of the other great success stories taking place at the same time at Holiday Inn headquarters was that of human resources. Like PR/communications, the HR department was undervalued. Truth was, due to some unfortunate employee relations outcomes under the previous management, some felt the department had proven more of a hindrance than a help. It was in need of an overhaul.

Here are some of the steps the department took to reposition itself:

- It began to function as a consultant, rather than a department of rules and regulations. To enable its team members to carry out the promise of being a resource and problem solver, management offered members lessons in "flawless consulting," a concept Peter Block presented in his 1978 book of the same name.
- The vice president of HR invested in a graphic identity, using color and graphic design to establish a consistent, highly recognizable image for HR. From this time on, all materials created by the department would incorporate this same professional design, making everything instantly recognizable as coming from HR.
- The department surveyed employees to find out how people felt and what they needed from HR.
- Based on the survey results, HR began to position information so that employees could understand how the company was contributing to bettering their lives. Instead of human resource gobbledy-gook (which is corporate gobbledy-gook cubed), benefits and wage and salary policies were written in plain English.
- At the same time, our PR group helped HR employees elevate the quality of their writing to be more interesting and infinitely more readable.

To borrow a thought from a country song, this was branding when branding wasn't cool. The department had a new image—one of action. It came across as more sophisticated, professional, and service-oriented than ever before. With enhanced credibility, it attracted better talent, which resulted in better management in areas such as benefits, compensation, and recruiting. Better, *more efficient* management freed up funds to do even more training and image building. One important result was that the recruiting team used more effective, targeted materials, representing the company overall more favorably and attracting new employees not just to HR but to all corporate departments.

It didn't happen overnight, but success built upon success. Within a year or so, the HR department began to look pretty attractive from the outside. Whereas other departments used to avoid getting HR involved in anything (for fear of encountering bureaucratic rules and delays), now they began to invite HR into their planning and problem-solving processes.

Years later, I had a chance to speak to someone who was, you might say, a target of internal marketing at the company. Angie Mock was at that time an auditor with Holiday Inns. She later went on to own a hospitality management company with 50 locations, where she put internal marketing to work as a change mechanism. Here's a story about how she became a true believer during those times.

"I learned early in my career the enormous value of internal marketing and communications," says Angie. "I spent the first ten years out of college with Holiday Inns, Inc. I'll never forget the first time I received a customized annual compensation summary. Although I had probably contemplated my *value* to the company, I had never really thought about what I *cost* the company. Almost 20 years later, I distinctly remember the wow effect of that neatly packaged and bound report with my name on the cover, outlining the total cost of my employment including salary, bonuses, health insurance, life insurance, 401(k) matching. I could have determined most of the information in the report from my pay stub, but because the company took the time and effort to show me clearly what I was worth to them, my loyalty factor shot straight to cloud nine."

BENEFITS OF MARKETING YOUR DEPARTMENT

What are some of the benefits that accrue from internal marketing D2D? Here are some that we've seen and experienced. You may:

- Reduce conflict with other departments.
- Establish relationships built on trust and form a base of valuable supporters in other areas of the company.
- Solve problems holistically with the help of other trusted resources.
- Attract better employees who recognize your department's status and want to work in it.
- Advance your ideas and plans with senior management and potentially increase your chances of receiving greater funding.
- Identify potential problems sooner through the feedback you get from unbiased sources.
- Contribute to other departments' projects in a meaningful way.
- Ultimately, be seen as a valuable factor in the organization's success.

Finally, internal marketing can help overcome the nasty politics that often come into play in a large company, or any company, for that matter. A cooperative atmosphere is more conducive to productivity. Harmonious relationships reduce stress for employees. Honesty and openness lead to the free flow of ideas. All of which lead ultimately to a better experience for the person on the receiving end of the relationships—your customer.

AND NOW THE DARK SIDE

Some years ago, I was involved in reengineering an orientation program for an organization that was essentially operating in the Dark Ages compared to the typical *Fortune* 500 company. This project goes down in history as one of the most frustrating of my career.

Sometime around 1990, the president of this company had asked the vice president of the HR department to evaluate and revitalize the new-hire orientation program.

After a year, tired of waiting and unwilling to hold the vice president accountable, the president picked a committee of 25 people from all disciplines to revamp the program. He assigned a high-potential, maverick manager to lead the effort. Perhaps I should rephrase that: The president took the project from HR and hung it like an anvil around the new project manager's neck. "Maverick," as I'll call him, was stuck with an unwieldy committee, along with the bad juju of a humiliated HR guy.

Because the department head was the epitome of what was holding the organization back—being mired in the mud of "we've always done it this way"—absolutely nothing had happened.

Enter the poor, unsuspecting consultant—me—dressed in an "I'll save the day" suit. Inspired by the brilliant and forward-thinking maverick manager, I was ready to rock and roll. But imagine 25 people meeting weekly via a rudimentary teleconferencing system. It was a miserable free-for-all that lasted two long, arduous hours. You could cut the territoriality with a knife. The bottom line was that no two people could agree at any given time. In desperation, I set about interviewing committee members individually, trying to take their ideas and compress those into a cohesive plan (a bit like stuffing a size 9 foot into a size 6 shoe).

Throughout this ordeal, the human resource manager we worked with was complaining that she didn't want to upset her boss, the vice president. She would play along with us, and then turn around and report back to him what terrible things we were doing. His reaction was to take no role in it, preferring instead to be obstructive.

We held in our hands such great power—the power to affect a new hire's feelings about her new organization, her excitement about her new position, and her ability to find the bathroom on her first day at work. It was a challenge to which I felt personally committed. I could perform a great service for the new hires and please the brilliant project manager. We had clicked, and I was hoping to work on other projects with him.

Naãve as I was in those days, I took the whole thing seriously, thinking we could pull it off. I stirred in the project manager's ideas, threw in a bit of my own knowledge of what makes employees tick, added two dashes of the committee's thoughts, and let it all simmer. Soon we had a workable solution; not perfect, but definitely a step in the right direction. Now it was time to see if it was palatable to the organization.

Before we went public, we wanted the organization's 60 top managers from multiple locations to buy in. We planned a trial run, and we invited the HR vice president to introduce the program to the group. The glory was his for the taking.

The project leader, along with another significant (and intelligent) team member, would do a word-for-word run-through. At the scheduled rehearsal time the day before the show, the HR guy came into the room bellowing about how one of the posters was too small. He promptly left, avoiding rehearsal entirely. I was impressed with his ability to focus on minutia.

As you would expect, the next day at the meeting, the vice president was embarrassingly ill-prepared. He read from some crumpled yellow note pages and stood for most of the time with his back to the group. It was one of the strangest performances I've ever seen. Fortunately, he was the first to speak, and there was a lot of time and good material between him and the end of the presentation. In spite of his antics, the group was pleased.

One facet of this program I haven't touched on is that the new orientation program was to be delivered the same way in 17 different facilities. Obviously, we had to train the trainers. The original plan had been for me to assist with the train-the-trainer program and then turn it all over to the HR group. I was intimately familiar with every aspect of the required information, as well as the fun stuff, and I could teach not only the letter but also the spirit of the program to the people who would have to deliver it out in the field. And this is where the biggest snag of all occurred. The human resources vice president, who had refused all our attempts to include him in the process, decided a manager from his department should run train-the-trainer sessions, even though she had no idea how to do it.

I explained to Maverick how concerned I was. He said, "We've done all we can do. Eventually, they're going to have to own this program, so they might as well start now. I've completed my assignment for the president."

Smart guy. It was time to cut bait because the fish was already dangling from a hook. So the HR group did all the training. I collected my fee and left. From the project, I gained the ongoing friendship of the project manager, who ended up running an entire business unit. A few years after the incident, he told me that the outlying facilities never embraced the program and the headquarters program did indeed go belly up.

This is a perfect example of the opposite of D2D marketing. When one department prefers to work in isolation, hog the credit, and avoid taking feedback from others, disaster is just around the corner. And in this case, the losing player is the new employee, who never has a chance to learn about the company's goals.

Chapter 9

TORCHBEARERS

Rewards and Recognition

You may wonder why we're dedicating a whole chapter to rewards and recognition. Hey, it's simple, right? Someone does a good job, you say thank you. You congratulate them in front of their peers. You may even give them a trophy if it's a very big deal. And sometimes, you might give a cash award, a trip, or some other valuable item in recognition of their work. When it comes time for their annual evaluation, they may even get a bigger raise.

You'd think it would be easy to say thanks for a great job, but many organizations struggle with this notion. Why, you ask? Like parents, some organizations are overtly "grateful" and some are not. Worst case, some companies feel, "Sure, what you did yesterday was good, but what are you gonna do for us today?"

Some common misconceptions exist that lead some organizations to believe that thanking their employees is too time-consuming and costly. But rewarding and recognizing the contributions of your employees doesn't have to happen at an annual awards banquet or involve a large bonus paycheck. We'll talk about some innovative ways that organizations can use rewards and recognition to internally market to their employees.

THE RULES OF REWARDS AND RECOGNITION

Even with the best of intentions, rewarding and recognizing can be ineffective if you don't follow some basic rules. For example, let's pretend your department has just completed a three-month project. As a reward, you send each of your employees a gift certificate in the inter-office mail for a free pizza and video rental—a relatively inexpensive but nice gesture, and something they can take home and share with their families. But this small reward for a job well done could have a larger impact on your employees.

Just imagine that your department is halfway through the large project and has to stay late one night to meet an important deadline. At the end of the night, you pass out the pizza and video gift certificates and say, "Thank you all so much for your dedication to meet this deadline. We recognize the sacrifice and choice you made to spend additional time at the office today, and hope you can use and share these certificates with your families as a token of our appreciation." That personal touch goes a long way.

For recognition and rewards to be most effective, they should be *sincere* and *timely*. Don't wait until a long and arduous project is completed before you thank the team members for a job well done. By using rewards and recognition along the way, you can keep morale high and improve employee loyalty. In the example above, immediate and sincere recognition for a completed deadline will show your employees that your organization appreciates them. And while the reward isn't a large one, employees will appreciate getting something unexpected delivered by someone in charge.

While rewarding and recognizing employees is necessary, you don't want to set a precedent that you can't maintain. Employees respond positively to unexpected and immediate rewards, but the effect of bonus checks given several times a year can begin to wear off (not to mention create a financial strain on your organization). Make sure you're combining your use of rewards with adequate recognition. A simple acknowledgment of an employee's hard work at a staff meeting can also be extremely effective.

REINFORCEMENT: THE FRAMEWORK

Imagine you are a gymnast training for the Olympics. You want to do a good job in every area, but specifically, you want to focus your energy on perfecting the areas that the judges will critique. But what if you don't know the judging criteria? What if they won't tell you, yet they keep handing out medals to the other gymnasts, leaving you to guess what you've missed? It would be very hard to maintain your determination to win that medal. After all, you could be wasting your time trying to perfect a technique that the judges thought was satisfactory. How frustrating!

And so it is with employee recognition programs. If you don't outline the rules, employees won't understand what they're striving for, and therefore, can be left hanging.

There are no right and wrong answers. The Olympic judges would be well within their rights to give higher priority to one exercise versus another, as long as they made it known ahead of time. They certainly couldn't switch mid-Olympics. However, we've heard from employees that they've felt exactly like priorities were constantly shifting based on the most recent "hot button" of the current supervisor. This is often tied to a poorly developed or narrow vision.

You simply must decide the fundamentals of your program and then communicate the guidelines before the program begins. You certainly don't want to find yourself in a situation where an employee believes he was unfairly cheated out of an award that was rightfully his, especially when you are aiming to motivate and encourage. The following sections detail the basic decisions you need to make regarding your recognition program.

Whom Are You Recognizing?

In general, we'd suggest that employees "compete" within their peer group: line-level employees rewarded among line-level employees, supervisors among supervisors. You can select winners locally, regionally, nationally—whatever fits your organization's design.

Will You Focus on Measurable Criteria and/or Subjective Factors?

Will you reward the person who gets the most customer compliments or will you consider the quality of the employee's actions? Is your winner going to be the person with the highest sales, or will you factor customer satisfaction into your equation? The most effective way to judge is to base criteria on your organization's goals, and then develop a clear-cut way of measuring how well employees carry them out.

It's frustrating to managers who try to do a good job of recognizing performance when employees who don't "win" complain about the "unfairness" of the program. To avoid that perception, set up your criteria in advance and make them very public. Of course, if you involve employees in the design of the process, they'll have even more ownership. Besides, it's hard to complain about something you created.

How Will You Communicate Your Selection Criteria?

Have you ever seen one of those entry forms that states the rules in teeny tiny type on the back of the nomination form? Don't make your employees work so hard to find out how you want them to behave. Make your criteria public and then reinforce, reinforce, reinforce. Just because *you've* heard it a thousand times doesn't mean that an employee understands. The greater the variety of your communication vehicles, the better. Say it in print, put up posters, make a verbal announcement, or send an e-mail. Use all your available resources.

How Will You Accept Employee Submissions?

The name of the game is Make It Easy. Consider the resources of your target audience. If you are collecting submissions from your maintenance staff—people who are not often exposed to an office environment—e-mail and fax would not be vehicles. Make sure that your submission forms are accessible and easy to understand.

Who Will Decide the Winner?

If your criteria are 100 percent measurable, deciding is easy. The person who has the highest score, most nominations, or best product wins. If you are considering subjective factors, that's another story. You'll need an impartial judge or judges, someone who is involved enough to understand the job situations, but removed enough to avoid playing favorites. A special committee can also work well.

Here's a word of warning. We once oversaw a manager of the year contest in which employees filled out nominations for their favorite manager from any department in the division. As the ballots were opened and read, we began to notice that a lot of the handwriting looked remarkably the same. When we had tallied up about 50 votes for the same manager, written in the same hand, we decided we were justified in saying that someone had stuffed the ballot box. Just something to consider: Design the nomination process so that this can't happen to you.

How Often Will You Recognize/Reward?

There is no such thing as too much recognition, as long as it's genuine and well-deserved. We encourage you to have many spontaneous moments of thanking people and patting them on the back every week. You can always find something to compliment someone on each and every day.

On top of these "quick hits," you may want to set up a regularly scheduled program. Common methods are monthly awards that lead to quarterly winners, or even annual winners. The most effective models are consistent. A program loses its impact if it's not implemented at its scheduled time.

A DIFFERENT KIND OF RECOGNITION

A few years ago, Angie Mock started her own hotel management company, Flagstone Hospitality Management. The new company was a spinoff, so much of the operational framework was in place—3,000 employees in 50 locations with existing processes and culture.

In our opinion, when she took over the culture was decidedly blah. As a high-energy person with a very charismatic personality, Angie was in a prime situation to mold the character of the organization. And her idea of culture was hands-on, team-oriented, open book.

To make it clear that she wanted to understand everyone's roles, she began by working different jobs in the hotels. Housekeepers were astounded when she showed up in a uniform and began scrubbing toilets and making beds. Throughout the day, she talked with employees and found out what they felt was important about their jobs, how they could better serve guests, and what they needed to make their jobs easier.

Angie also took a formal approach to getting employee input. She brought people from every level of the organization to a meeting where they talked about what kind of company they wanted to work for. The culture would be built by the employees. So, from that meeting, seven values emerged.

Angie communicated the seven values to her team, starting at the top. She told her executive team, "We're going to manage the company by these [values]. Whenever there's a question about a decision we might make, we'll let our values guide us."

To explain her philosophy and goals to the hotel managers, she held a kickoff conference to meet everyone and share plans. What a shock! The day began with a hot rock and roll band, at one point accompanying the seven senior executives as they sang "Heard It through the Grapevine." Not a pretty site, we assure you, but certainly an effective way to demonstrate one of her values—communication.

One assignment during the conference was for small groups to write and perform songs about the seven values. Compositions ranged from a rap song to a marching band and cheerleading squad. It was a memorable day, a barrel of fun, and a smart way to burn the values into their memories.

After that kickoff, Angie had plastic pins made, each one printed with a word for one of the values. When she visited the hotels, or walked around the corporate office, she carried the pins in her pocket. When she saw or heard an employee doing something that exemplified a value, she gave that person a pin, on the spot.

Never think that recognition has to be expensive and showy. The people who earned those pins treasured them as if they were solid gold.

Look at the many ways Angie recognized the employees:

- She showed that she valued them by asking for their input.
- She did their job, demonstrating that every person's contribution is important.
- She took the time to communicate the messages all the way up and down the organization.
- She used immediate reinforcement when she saw good performance by handing out the pins, simultaneously modeling the behavior of recognition for the managers and senior executives.

This is what we mean when we say walk the talk. She lived the philosophy, showing others what it looked like, and helping them understand what she expected of them.

What we've just described may not fall under the traditional means of recognition. Yet it worked to make people feel special, proud, and successful. And it's important to establish the basics of this type of internal culture before you create a recognition program. You absolutely must have a foundation in place—no matter how you go about getting there—before your recognition efforts will be meaningful to your employees.

Of course, we're not suggesting you do it just as Angie Mock did, but it boils down to this: Employees must understand your vision, and know you are invested in making it happen.

OTHER FACTORS TO CONSIDER

Make sure the recognition is tied to your goals in ways employees understand. If an employee is not entirely sure what he or she did to deserve a reward, it's much less meaningful, and impossible to strive toward or recreate. A perfect example of this is the typical employee-of-the-month program. Yes, of course, there are times when the honor is tied to measurable performance goals. In car dealerships, for example, the person who sells the most cars becomes the employee of the month. But in many cases, selecting the honoree is actually no more defined than drawing a name from a hat.

Employees value recognition they've strived to achieve much more than a random spotlight. So if you use an employee-of-the-month-type program, be sure the employees know what the qualifications are and that the qualifications match your overall goals.

If your goal is customer satisfaction, then reward employees who get fantastic customer comment cards or outstanding scores on customer surveys. If, as a company, you strive for high sales, reward your top performers. The bottom line: Reward the behavior you want to promote.

Recognize Specific Behaviors to Reinforce Your Company's Vision.

Instead of saying, "I really appreciate what a great job you do," try saying "I really appreciate the way you took care of Mr. Jones when he had a problem with his account. You took the initiative to find a solution for him and that really supports our vision of 100 percent customer satisfaction."

But what if your employees don't know your vision? Tell them! Many employers make the mistake of thinking that employees won't care about the goal because their only concerns are picking up their paycheck and what time they go home. This just isn't the case. In most cases, people want to be a part of something meaningful. They will eagerly sign on to help you achieve your company vision as long as they know what it is.

Also, make sure you encourage employees to begin to think in terms of actions that support the overall goal. Years ago we wrote employee spotlights as part of a recognition program for a manufacturing company. The company took submissions from peers and selected a winner each month. It was amazing how many entries said very kind, but very nondescript things like: She does anything it takes. She really goes the extra mile. He always helps out. Volume is not always about great performance; it can represent popularity. And while the sheer volume of submissions for some award recipients can be impressive, they pale in comparison to a nomination that tells a really great story with the specifics of a situation. To help guide employees in their submission styles, try using a form such as this:

I, _____, nominate _____ to win the [*award name here*] because: _____
_____.

I believe this supports our mission to [*fill in with your message*] because: _____
_____
_____.

Not only does this give you a chance to reinforce your message, but also it helps employees focus their thoughts on the organization's values as they are writing the submissions.

THE BIG QUESTION: WHAT'S THE REWARD?

Saying thanks one-on-one is always important. And because you can do it immediately, this method is a really fantastic way to recognize a job well done—as long as it doesn't end there.

PDAs: Public Displays of Appreciation Are Essential

There are many ways you can take recognition beyond the personal "attaboy." Here are a few. Don't feel like you have to use only one—pick several!

- Post winners' names and/or photos on a bulletin board in the break area.
- Write a "spotlight" for the company publication.

- Present an award at a company gathering or corporate meeting.
- Decorate the winner's cubicle or office space.
- Have winners wear a special pin or ribbon.
- E-mail a compliment to the employee, copying his team members, supervisor, or another company leader.

Reinforce your message with spontaneous, informal gestures. This would include taking an employee to lunch, sending flowers or a gift, or letting her go home an hour early.

Combine the personal, immediate thank you or informal gesture with a public display of appreciation and a meaningful reward, and what you've got is a sure-fire formula for skyrocketing employee morale and loyalty.

There is one exception to this rule: Be sensitive to employees' preferences and personality differences. Some people claim they don't like the spotlight, but secretly enjoy it. Others are truly shy and don't like to have attention drawn to them. You know your employees. If it would make them feel awkward to receive a public display of appreciation, find an alternative way to reward and recognize them within their comfort zone.

BEYOND THE TROPHY

Pins and trophies are a great permanent reminder of an achievement and they are a mainstay of recognition (not to mention a valuable photo-op). There's still no substitute for giving an employee something they can use for personal enjoyment. Extra time off and bonuses are obviously popular. Another big favorite is a company perk that goes beyond the customary employee discount.

Travel and leisure companies (airlines, hotels, cruises, etc.) can offer their employees a handsome frequent flyer points reward system so they can earn free trips, just as their customers do when they fly and stay at hotels. We especially recommend using this idea as part of recognition and rewards program to encourage service excellence and other performance indicators.

Retail companies (fashion, electronics, and a hundred other types) usually offer employee discounts. In addition to this, we suggest company competitions for product designs, advertising, and other creative ideas that involve all employees, so they feel closer to the customer-focused elements of the company. This has also proven a powerful way to drive innovation.

Fashion, music, and entertainment companies have the great advantage of offering their employees access to cool, trendy events and venues. SoundExchange, a small nonprofit organization in Washington, D.C., can't afford to pay its employees as much as some private companies, but it more than makes up for it by taking advantage of its place in the music industry. SoundExchange regularly gives away free concert passes to its employees and even holds private lunch concerts featuring upcoming new artists that it represents. Because most of its employees are major music fans, they love the trade-off.

Professional services companies (law, medicine, banking, consulting) have the disadvantage of not having a tangible product to give away, but they have the advantage of providing some of the most sought-after and valuable services in any industry. It may sound like a strange "perk," but giving your employees the on-the-job time to offer pro-bono services is an excellent way of promoting a sense of pride and contribution that comes straight from the core of their job. It also sends the message that your company cares about them and their fulfillment, and it has the extraordinary benefit of actually giving back to the community and helping people!

Nonprofit companies have an inherent disadvantage compared to for-profit companies when it comes to the amount they can afford to pay their employees. But they have an inherent advantage in the emotional commitment of their employees. Employees of nonprofit companies generally choose to work there for personal, emotional reasons that go beyond a paycheck, and nonprofits can capitalize on this with little effort.

On-the-spot awards are also great motivators. At many companies, employees and managers get slips to hand out to others they see doing a good job, exhibiting teamwork, or and going above and beyond. After the person earns a certain number of slips, they may turn them in for movie certificates, T-shirts, or other gifts. Who wouldn't want a reward of his or her choosing? This goes a long way in motivating employees on a day-to-day basis and is a good tool for rewarding on-the-spot behaviors. Don't wait until an annual dinner to recognize your employees for how well they're doing. Do it now!

Brand Smart: Take Advantage of Your Industry

If you ran a beer company, how would you make your employees feel more connected to your brand? With beer, perhaps? That's an easy answer if your business is beer, but we think there are creative ways of linking your employees to your brand no matter what type of business you're in. With that said, running a beer company does have its perks when it comes to brewing up loyalty and passion among your "beery" cheery staff. So let's visit Boston Beer Company.

According to George Orwell, 1984 was supposed to be the year that Big Brother took control of the world. Instead, it was the year Jim Koch started brewing beer in his Boston kitchen. Beer lovers consider 1984 to have been a very good year.

He introduced his home brew, Samuel Adams, to 20 bars in 1985. Six weeks later, Samuel Adams was named The Best Beer in America at the Great American Beer Festival. Today it's the sixth-largest brewery and the recipient of more awards than any other beer company—over 650 in its modest history. It's also one of the greatest brands of beer today.

How did the company get there? Jim Koch might tell you it took a whole lot of determination (he certainly had the door slammed in his face many times when he started out) and the help of some great people. But it also took a lot of smart thinking on his part to get those great people to feel as passionately about his beer as he did.

Jim created a sort of combination training-reward-morale-booster contest that tied directly to the beer. It led him to give his employees the chance to brew their own beer.

"Now we hold an annual homebrew competition," says Jim, "where every employee is challenged to develop an original recipe and brew a batch of beer. This tradition recalls the first batch of Samuel Adams Boston Lager that I brewed in my kitchen more than 20 years ago."

While peer pressure is a mighty motivator, nothing gets people into their special brews like the grand prizes. Every year the three grand prize winners each win an all-expenses-paid trip for two to Germany for Oktoberfest. And just so bragging rights are intact at the company's annual meeting in January, all three winning recipes are brewed up for the whole company to share.

Here are a few other interesting homebrew contest facts:

- Employees who choose not to create an alcoholic beverage in their homes are invited to submit root beer recipes, and often the product development for these becomes a family affair.
- According to the Samuel Adams brewing staff, which judges the competition, the quality (as well as the quantity) of the submissions has increased dramatically over the years.
- This year 75 percent of the company's employees submitted one or more beers to the competition.
- Three years ago the entire company embarked on an integrated new team-building program. The employees were divided into 16 interdepartmental groups (named after the styles of beer the company sells). Today, while the winners are individual, the teams are judged according to their lev-

els of participation. This means employees are encouraged by their peers to participate.
- While the annual homebrew competition is still the biggest event, there are similar team competitions for innovative marketing ideas and for beer haiku.
- The annual company meeting is a rich tapestry of activities, some educational, some social, some team building, and some just "rip-roaring fun."

Okay, so you're thinking it's easy to create a fun, inspiring internal brand and "rip-roaring fun" when your business is beer, but what if your business is manufacturing or health care? Some industries may not lend themselves as easily to branding because of the nature of their business, but we believe it's always possible to find creative ways to leverage your specific industry to build your internal brand and connect with your employees. Here are some examples:

- A trucking firm could hold an annual truck "rodeo" for drivers, complete with western gear and music.
- A hospitality company could hold a bed-making competition, or a vacuum cleaner race.

Every spring, Memphis, Tennessee, has its annual Memphis in May event, a month-long celebration when the city highlights its heritage of music, food, art, and other distinctly Memphis fare. Over the years, the city has included a number of competitive events such as the Great Wine Race, in which bar or restaurant servers race carrying a tray of glasses full of wine. It's a sloppy and fun time. Is it obvious where we're going with this? If you owned a restaurant in Memphis, you might want to recognize your best server by sponsoring them in the race. What better way to show you value their skill?

In another innovative contest, corporate teams show off their culinary skills in the World Championship Barbecue Cooking Contest. Recognized in the 1999 Guinness Book of World

Records as the largest pork barbecue contest in the world, the three-day event attracts around 100,000 people and remains the unchallenged leader in this delicious category. Teams from all over the country compete for top prizes in showmanship and cooking (whole hog, shoulder and ribs, and so on).

How does this relate to employee recognition and rewards? We all know that recognition inside a company is important and highly effective in making employees feel proud. External recognition is another means by which you can showcase your employees and develop their pride as members of your team.

For the barbecue contest, corporations around the city sponsor cooking teams. Winners are featured in local news outlets. Better yet, they become part of history and contribute to publicity that has in the past included a spot on a Food Network show—a 30-minute prime-time special hosted by Al Roker—as well as *Good Morning America, Today, CBS This Morning,* and national attention in publications including *Smithsonian, New Yorker, USA TODAY,* and the *Wall Street Journal.*

Sharing Ownership

Seth Goldman put his high-flying finance career and Harvard and Yale degrees to good use. He started making tea. Not just any tea, though—Honest Tea. The company is deeply rooted in an environmentally friendly, health conscious philosophy, and Seth takes every opportunity to reinforce those values in his branding—both inside and out.

Seth is a big believer in making employees feel a sense of ownership, and his strategies have paid off. Honest Tea offers the usual dose of employee stock options so they can become literal shareholders of the company. But it also uses a more creative—and free—method of giving employees a sense of ownership.

"On every bottle of tea is a UPC code," says Seth, describing the ten-digit bar code that uniquely identifies products. "We can choose the last five digits, which identify the product. Most companies just select numbers in sequence, but we let our employees choose the numbers, so it becomes *their* product. People like to choose their birthday or their anniversary, and they really feel a sense of ownership for that product, and, therefore, for the company."

He tells the story of one employee who lost his father. "We didn't tell him ahead of time, but when we launched a new product, we made the UPC code his father's birthday. When he saw it, he was so overwhelmed. You better believe that he has really strong feelings about the success of that product, and the success of the company as a whole."

It goes to show that there are very simple, inexpensive ways to show your employees that you care and make them feel connected to your brand.

Overcoming Obstacles

Recently I had occasion to do a focus group with about ten managers to find out how they recognize employees. One manager expressed his frustration. "If I recognized one employee for outstanding performance, the others get jealous. It's caused so much friction, I figure I'm better off not recognizing anyone at all."

We were horrified when we heard that, yet we could also understand. We live in a strange world where justice and fairness are big issues. Everyone seems to feel that they are entitled to whatever someone else gets, even if they did nothing to earn it. The "sense of entitlement" mentality is a thorn in the side of managers, who develop resentment. They try to give their employees a positive environment, but every time they try, they receive nothing but criticism. No wonder they give up.

Several years ago, I was in that position myself. For months, my partner and I had worked to revamp a toxic customer service department. This department was so toxic that the poison was leaking out all over customers. In one instance, an employee felt perfectly justified in retaliating against a customer who complained. She called the customer a very, very inappropriate name, and even called the customer back several times to harass her. Needless to say, it had been a long six months. But things didn't get screwed up overnight, and they wouldn't be easily fixed.

We talked with employees, carefully examined the environment, discovered things that were indeed unfair, and worked with management to address employees' issues. We literally rebuilt the department, and now it was time to unveil the plan.

One of the strategies we employed was that of building pride. Because their jobs were to rebuild relationships with customers, we called the group "Goodwill Ambassadors." We gave them T-shirts with that designation, explaining how important they are to the company's success. It was just one of many small things we did to recast their role from complaint takers to satisfaction creators.

Along with the many changes designed to make things better for employees, we also put in place consequences. For quite some time, employees had ignored the official 8:00 AM start time, ambling in at their convenience. (Because the department also employed a night shift, latecomers caused the night workers to have to stay longer. Pretty unfair on their part, but they didn't see it from that perspective.) They also took advantage of the lunch hour and breaks. We needed to demonstrate the quid pro quo of a fair workplace: We do what's right for you, and you do what's right for us.

When we announced a new demerit system for tardiness, they immediately thought up outlandish situations that could be considered exceptions to the rule. Their goal was to find the loopholes in the system. One person said, "Well, what if there's an electrical storm and my power is out and I can't open my garage door? Why should I get a demerit?" We suggested a cab. "What if I can't get a cab in time?" And so the discussion went. These employees were hell bent on believing that someone was trying to cheat them out of something.

It would be easy to blame these employees and to become disheartened about trying to change things. If you are consistent and you walk the talk, your team will either get on board or they will leave.

Recognizing the Greater Good

Keep in mind that just because an employee receives a paycheck, it does not mean that he finds fulfillment within the workplace. Often, the number on a paycheck holds very little meaning if an employee does not receive any personal satisfaction from work. Each person makes a choice to leave her family each day and come to work at your organization. If she can walk down the street for the same paycheck, what's keeping her loyal to your company?

Years ago when I was working at Holiday Inn, the University of Memphis Tigers basketball team made it to the Final Four playoffs. The entire city was excited about the game, and the employees at Holiday Inn were able to get in on the action. On the day of the game, we took the afternoon off and threw a huge pep rally at the office. Departments held contests with each other for the best decorating—some put tiger paw prints on the floor and transformed the office with the team's colors. You couldn't help but get in on all of the excitement, even if you weren't a big basketball fan.

To this day, I don't remember which team won, but what I do still recall is how much fun we had rallying around the basketball team. Community involvement can help boost morale and provide a real treat for your employees.

FedEx is well known for donating much of its time and money to community relations. One of its largest charitable drives is for the March of Dimes, an organization that funds research and aid for premature childbirth. The annual WalkAmerica campaign asks participants to gather contributions from their friends and families for a walk, and companies often match the dollar amount that each employee raises for the event. Last year, over 11,000

FedEx employees participated in the fund-raiser and walk. Because premature childbirth is so common, many employees have been touched by the problem, and they rally around the charity because it strikes a personal chord.

So how do community relations events relate to internal marketing? When your employees see they work for an organization that promotes community efforts and allows them to use company resources toward the greater good, they are likely to feel a greater loyalty for both the organization and the community. Employees that might not ordinarily donate their free time or money to a charity often join their coworkers and find both personal and professional fulfillment in their newfound involvement. It's a win-win situation for both your organization and the community.

Several years ago, Homewood Suites developed a unique program called "Driving Literacy Home." The corporate office challenged its hotel teams to collect thousands of books to donate to children. Anyone could contribute. At the end of the campaign, an 18-wheel truck with a Homewood Suites campaign banner designed on the side drove from coast to coast, stopping at each Homewood Suites hotel to pick up the books. Not only were the employees able to participate in their own local book collections, but they were actually able to peer into the back of the truck and see the impact that an entire organization can have on a community!

The media loved the campaign, so the company benefited from the publicity. Better yet, employees of the hotels saw their company featured in local and national newspapers. Their sense of accomplishment was magnified by the visibility.

Internally, the groups that participated earned recognition via a giant scrapbook. Each team submitted photos from their book drive. Employees from Homewood Suites still fondly remember this campaign, and many still have small replicas of the truck sitting on their desks.

So what if your company is a very small organization that doesn't have thousands of employees? What sorts of things can you and your employees do to promote community relations?

- *"Adopt an Angel."* Choose an underprivileged child or family to "adopt" during the holiday season. Some organizations might even opt to forgo an annual Christmas party and use the money to buy presents and food.
- *Disaster relief.* Has a local storm damaged your community or one close to you? Have a fundraiser for the storm victims and get your employees involved.

You, as a manager, must also be highly involved in the effort. Whether hosting a pep rally for your team or collecting money for underprivileged children, your employees must see that you are also committed to the cause.

Recognizing and rewarding your employees for their participation is also extremely important. Whether you put their names in the weekly newsletter or give out a prize to the person who raises the most money, show your appreciation for their efforts.

And, finally, don't forget to make it fun. One organization of which we know was trying to raise money for a local charity and held an Easter egg hunt inside of the office. Employees were asked to donate money to participate, and they were allowed to wear jeans on the day of the "hunt." When they arrived to work, everyone gathered outside so they could enter the office at the same time and search for the plastic eggs, which were hidden in cubicles, file cabinets, and office plants. The eggs were stuffed with candy and change, but the "golden egg" contained an extra day's vacation. You can bet that an egg hunt aimed at adults encouraged participation!

Chapter 10

TRUE LIFE SITUATIONS

You're familiar with the phrase too little, too late. Let me tell you a story that illustrates the expression.

Julie is married to Bob, a perfectly nice man who does not communicate with her. She makes it clear that this is an important issue, and she coaxes Bob to work with her. She suggests a variety of options they could consider to improve their communication—books, videotapes, seminars, counseling, and so on. He repeatedly resists and after quite a few years Julie finally says, "Bob, I'm out of here." He rushes out and buys some books. Maybe they'll come in handy with his next wife.

Internal marketing is a marriage with your employees. It's a way of building honest relationships that will carry you through good times and rocky ones. Just like in marriage, you can't afford to wait until the whole arrangement crumbles to pay attention to the partnership. You have to take preventive steps.

Internal marketing will make your organization more effective in its day-to-day operations. That's a fact. But you'll see the full impact of internal marketing when you face situations that are more global and serious; situations where change is required. These might be quality initiatives, mergers or acquisitions, responses to sudden industry downturns, disasters like September 11, or a host of other difficult times. During periods of uncertainty, you need your team focused on the job at hand, not worrying about whether you're telling them the truth or whether they'll be out of a job, or feeling paranoid about their teammates. If you have solid relationships already in place, your job will be much easier and your team will be more successful.

It sounds a bit melodramatic, but internal marketing can truly be the difference between success and failure.

In this chapter, we're going to share some true corporate adventures. Some follow the principles of internal marketing and some don't. Draw your own conclusions.

A MIDSIZE MERGER

Several years ago we were asked by a marketing firm to develop an internal communications plan for two companies that were merging. The two groups were midsized companies, each with a couple of hundred employees. They were creating a new entity, complete with a sparkling new brand identity.

This was an inspiring project for us because we had seldom seen companies make communications such an integral part of their plans for change. Even more surprising was that companies of this size and structure—they were both family businesses—would be wise enough to develop a serious communications plan, especially so early in the process.

During our first interviews, it became clear. These two groups were deeply concerned about what would be best for their employees in every regard, from where the headquarters would be located to what benefits they would offer. When it was time to make decisions, management was committed to doing the right thing for their people. And even if that meant a short-term business decision might be slightly less than ideal, they knew that in the long run their company would be healthier if they did what would engender trusting, satisfied employees. This principle guided everything we did.

Naturally, there were many components of this merger that we won't go into here. But we had intimate knowledge of the important plans below.

The first order of business was to announce the merger. The owners were adamant that they wanted employees to be the first to know, and they wanted to meet face to face with every single person. Our plan called for an employee meeting with the simultaneous issue of the press release.

To prepare the managers for the meeting, we created a presentation that outlined exactly what was happening. The emphasis was on how the merger would affect employees. Yes, it talked about how the merger would benefit the companies, but in this first session it was most important that management answer the employees' biggest question: How will it affect me? Management wanted to personally reassure each employee on an individual basis, and following the presentation, they were available to answer questions.

The process was quite easy at the headquarters location. But each of these companies had satellite offices. Still, management was absolutely determined to find a way that everyone could be informed simultaneously so that no one would hear the news of the merger from an outside source or through the company grapevine.

As communications experts, we challenged ourselves to figure out how a manager could be in two places at once.

Faced with this type of situation, many companies would develop a plan for management's convenience. Not these guys. The two presidents said they wanted members of the highest level of management to go on the road to talk to employees at their satellite offices the same day the announcement was made. This meant driving several hours to reach all outlying areas. The five executives divvied up the locations so that they each were assigned an office where they would give the same presentation management had given at headquarters. They were also armed with FAQs. Knowing that employees' first reaction probably would be shock, we wrote a handout that employees could refer to later, and could also take home and share with their families. And we set up a hotline employees could call anytime during the several-month transition.

As the process played out, the new company published a weekly newsletter to keep everyone informed of the progress of moving offices, and so on. It was a well-orchestrated event, and it went smoothly.

Now here's the kicker: Even with a well-thought-out plan, never underestimate the potential for employees to be confused, scared, unsure, and otherwise unsettled about change. Take the following example as proof.

After the fact, one of the company presidents told us a story of how his eyes were opened during his drive to one of the satellite offices. He was accompanied by one of his key managers. We'll call him Pete. Pete was one of the managers enlisted to help with the transition. He was apprised of the situation before the employee meeting and assured that his job was completely secure. As they rode to the meeting, the president praised Pete for his good work and thanked him for coming along to help out. The president further explained that there would be a handful of employees whose jobs would end up being redundant, so they would have to be let go. He went on to talk about benefits packages and the process of integrating the two groups smoothly.

All was well, right? Get this: At the end of the trip, Pete looked at the president and said, "Am I going to be let go?"

The president was dumbstruck. Hadn't he told Pete face to face what a great job he had done, and that his job was safe? How could Pete think that the president would have him drive all around to inform other employees if Pete was going to be out of a job? And how did Pete interpret the president's words of praise? Hadn't Pete heard a word the president had said?

No matter how high up you go in an organization, every person involved in a drastic change will immediately think, "How does this affect me?" Until your employees' basic human needs for safety and security are met, they can't share your vision or excitement about the benefit to the company of this change.

Change calls for very simple and direct statements. If there are any negatives to the situation, don't try to soften the message with positioning, or sugarcoat it by telling everyone what a super job they've done. Vague statements mislead people and leave them guessing. At this point they want a simple declarative sentence, whether the news is happy or unhappy. Tell them, "You have a job" or "You don't have a job." That may seem harsh, but by telling it like it is you show respect for your employees and recognition of them as adults.

Finally, reinforce the message and *ask people if they understand what it means*.

In early communications, go easy on the details about how a move achieves the company's strategy. That can come later, after the initial shock, when people realize their jobs are not in jeopardy. And don't be surprised if people are skittish for a while. During times of change, many continue to wait for the other shoe to drop.

HOOK, LINE, AND SINKER

Fish where the fish are. That's what we did at M. S. Carriers.

In 1999, M. S. Carriers was the seventh largest truckload carrier in the country. Founded by Michael Starnes, it was highly successful in transporting freight.

Truck drivers comprised the majority of the company. They were an unusual employee audience to corral. This was not a group you could call into an auditorium for a presentation. Most were on the road, sometimes for ten days at a time, so it was difficult to get information to them in a timely way. Printed materials got some readership, but most were discarded in the break room.

Interestingly, a large percentage of the drivers were highly educated. They chose this profession because it allowed them to travel all over the country and be free of the confines of an office job.

I was originally hired to assist with benefits communication. My client, Lynn Lesher, was in charge of benefits and compensation, and she understood the need for targeted communication. The information she needed to communicate was, in many cases, legally required, making it essential that we deliver it on time and in a form that was understandable. Employees would make decisions about their health care options and other benefits as a result of what they read in these documents. Any change in benefits could dramatically affect a driver and his or her family. Lynn couldn't afford to take a hit-or-miss approach to employees receiving the information.

We worked together to create a plan that would suit a driver's needs. There were a number of challenges.

First, of course, was the fact that the drivers were on the road constantly. If we sent information to their homes, we could never be sure they would receive and read it. A week or so may go by before a driver returns home and it is certainly possible and even probable that during this gap in time, mail could be misplaced or discarded. And in the case of benefits information, the driver's spouse frequently was the one who read and dealt with any benefits changes or enrollment requirements. If the delivery required the employee's signature, receipt of the documents would be delayed until the driver returned home.

Second, because drivers spent their time driving, they weren't likely to read a lot of the company's print materials, even if the materials were about something as important as benefits.

Third, when drivers did come to the headquarters, they spent as little time there as possible. If anything, they used headquarters as a place to shower or sleep. Their attention span for reading company information during their stop at headquarters was pretty short.

Ultimately, we realized that the most important thing was to create such a desire for the information that they would seek out the documents from the home office. This approach required us to motivate the drivers by "selling" them on the great things the company's plan could offer rather than trying to present all the details in one document.

Still, we had to figure out how to reach them. Through print? No. Video? Not possible. Audio? A-ha! While they drove, the drivers listened to music, talk radio, and even books on tape. The solution became obvious—audiotapes. Drivers spend enough hours on the road to sing along with Garth Brooks, hum a Bach Fugue, and learn French in 12 easy lessons. We decided to capture a portion of their drive-time listening pleasure.

The challenge, however, was to not turn the benefits information audiotape into a sleep aid. Our goal was to develop a short, fun tape that would be very memorable. If the tape did its job, it would create top-line awareness and pique the drivers' interest to learn more. All we needed to accomplish was to convince them to seek more detailed information.

Trying to put ourselves in the drivers' seats, we decided that something entertaining would most likely get their attention. Humor was in order. We wrote a script that took place on the median of an interstate highway. A state trooper stopped Lynn for posting signs about new benefits. We hired a local actor to play the trooper. Lynn played herself, acting so excited about the new company benefits that she just couldn't stop herself from telling the world.

Short and sweet, the recorded message got the point across, and, better still, it could be replayed without being onerous or boring. We followed it up with a print package that went into more detail, which we mailed to their homes.

The tool worked because we fished where the fish were.

There are some guidelines to follow when you're deciding how to deliver information. In many cases, you may choose to use multiple vehicles to reinforce each other. The trick is to honor different people's methods of absorbing information. Some of us are visual, some are tactile, and some prefer audio. Regardless of the preferred method of receiving information, the vast majority of us retain information best if we see it, hear it, feel it, and, when appropriate, use it.

YOU HAVE TO CRACK SOME EGGS

Perkins Restaurants is a family-style restaurant chain with locations primarily in Minnesota, Pennsylvania, Ohio, Florida, and Wisconsin. It employs about 25,000 people at 500 company-owned or franchised full-service restaurants.

One of our projects at Perkins related to employee benefits at the company-owned stores. While the company offered a good benefits package, few store employees signed up for it. Because Perkins wanted to use benefits as a competitive advantage in recruiting for these jobs, it was concerned about increasing its employee participation levels. The company challenged its HR director to increase enrollment.

Working on this kind of project is a lot like being a detective. First you have to find out why people aren't using the benefits. Your initial thought might be, "We need to better publicize benefits," or "We need to do a better job explaining benefits so employees can understand them." Those were our suspicions when we began. It appeared to be a simple matter of better "advertising."

Luckily, we didn't act on those assumptions because they were absolutely wrong. Upon deeper investigation, we discovered something we couldn't have predicted. When managers looked at their profit and loss statements each month, they saw a line indicating that they were paying X amount for their employees' benefits. The stores' profitability affected the managers' bonuses. Because they viewed benefits as an expense that would potentially decrease their bonuses, they weren't eager to get employees to sign up. They saw benefits as an area in which they could save money that would lead to better end-of-year results. Therefore, managers did not communicate much about benefits to the employees, and they certainly didn't encourage enrollment.

In truth, there was quite a gap between what the store managers thought and what was actually happening. The reality was that the benefits line item was zeroed out at the end of the year, meaning that it did not affect the bottom line or the manager's bonus. Thus, the solution to our problem was not to better communicate benefits to employees; it was to explain to managers that the benefits didn't affect their P&L.

Using that approach, we created a series of postcards that showcased how benefits would make it easier for these store managers to attract and retain better employees, thus creating a competitive advantage. It was a great internal marketing opportunity. We identified the correct audience (managers, not employees), defined their needs (better bonuses), and tailored the communication to show how benefits helped the manager (better recruiting equals more effective employees).

Once we cleared up confusion about how the benefits affected the bottom line, and showed the managers it would actually help them, not hurt them, we saw an immediate turnaround. Following the communication, there was a 30 percent increase in store employee enrollment during the next benefits enrollment period.

TWO ORGANIZATIONS SAVE A PENNY, SPEND A MILLION

In the late 1980s and early 1990s, a big chunk of American businesses began furiously waving the "quality" banner. Amazingly, it seemed that quality was not the norm in business at that time. It was no longer something that buyers could take for granted. When buying a product (or service), customers made no assumption of quality. We're all accustomed to being asked "Would you like fries with that?" when we pull up to the drive-thru at McDonald's, but imagine buying a new car and being asked, "Would you like quality with that?" As a result, companies began using their advertising campaigns to not only showcase their product but also to promise it was a quality product. Egad.

Quality became the goal for which all companies were striving. In 1987, they tried becoming certified in ISO 9000 standards. They sought the Malcolm Baldridge Award. They joined quality associations. And those of us in the writing business wrote tag lines like: Quality Is Job 1.

Around this time, we were associated with two companies that initiated quality programs. Although we've promoted internal branding as the be-all, end-all of employee focus and motivation, we want to admit that in some cases companies can accomplish something without it. (After all, quite a number of companies have managed to make money without even knowing what internal marketing is!)

The first of these two companies is a financial institution with multiple locations. About ten years ago or so it adopted a catchy slogan, defined what quality meant to the company, and hired a top-notch training group to create workshops for its thousands of employees. The sessions included marvelously colored flip charts, fun games, and guidelines for quality standards and how to reach them. It was a million-dollar project that took months to plan and execute.

We were on the periphery, but we're not known for keeping our noses out of other people's business. We couldn't help but ask whether they had plans for a communication program to reinforce the one-time training. It seemed to us that although employees were excited about the effort, they weren't 100 percent sure how to implement quality in their own jobs. Certain aspects were very clear; others, confounding. We felt there was additional work to be done in communicating practical, step-by-step directions, and that ongoing suggestions, recognition, and reinforcement would be necessary.

By then, however, the budget had all been spoken for, and full-blown communications were not a part of it. Despite our urging, the leaders were unable to consider incorporating that type of reinforcement.

After about a year, we spoke to the head of the quality project about its success. She felt that some things were becoming second nature to employees. Certainly the slogan was still known, and the core of the concept of working toward quality was in place. She also said that they could now see how important regular communication was in the equation, and that they felt they had not been successful at that aspect.

Ten years later, the slogan and core principles are still at work in the company. But it's a bit different than they originally intended. Luckily for the company, it does a better job of walking the talk than talking. It has an outstanding organization, and is still considered a tremendously positive place to work. Its financial performance and employee retention are excellent. But think what it might have been with the extra boost of sustained internal marketing.

• • • • •

The second quality rally we observed was at a health care institution. When we learned of its quality initiative we were doing consulting work in another area of the company, and so were invited to attend some of their "quality circles." We saw immediately that the plan was riddled with holes. First, the company's definition of quality was extremely difficult to understand. Second, its method of explaining quality to employees was not methodical or well planned. Third, it hadn't planned any reinforcement through accountability, any recognition of those who did it right, or any communication beyond the kickoff.

By the time we were invited to this meeting, the plan was underway. Naturally, from the outside, it was easy to see what was happening, and the news was not good. As bona fide capitalists, we enjoy getting paid for what we do. In this case, however, we were driven by the need to help because "they knew not that they knew not." Although we hadn't been hired to assist in this area, once again we felt compelled to save the company from itself. We offered suggestions which were met with resistance. It's hard to sit back and watch clients fail.

Within months, the initiative was floundering. Two different departments were in a pitch battle for ownership of it. Employees didn't understand it. Management seemed satisfied that they had at least done something, but, unfortunately, it did nothing to improve the organization.

Some years later we were hired by this same company to help with—you guessed it—quality issues. As they say, pay now or pay later.

Without a cohesive, comprehensive plan to support such an initiative, it's just about guaranteed to fizzle.

DON'T BE A FIRELESS LEADER

In 2003, business sadism hit TV in the form of *The Apprentice*. Come one, come all. Watch businessman and grandstander Donald Trump vet potential employees and discharge losers with the invective, "You're fired!" Only Trump could make people love those two words. Only he could get millions of viewers to tune in week after week to watch him publicly criticize and humiliate would-be Trumps. Only he could instill loyalty with nastiness and greed at its core. It's not pretty, but you've got to admit he's has the power to fire people up.

But even reality television can't hold a candle to internal marketing when it comes to creating loyal fans. The minute a plotline drags or a series kills off a popular character, viewers will jump to the next hot series like that. Snap! This won't happen with employees who've got the fire. Remember the Holiday Inn employees? They stood by the company when its stock dropped to $4 a share. They stayed enthusiastic when the company took a beating with its failed attempts at restaurant concepts. Even after many of the employees were laid off as a result of the company's move from Memphis to Atlanta, they attended reunions for another 15 years. That is what diehard loyalty looks like.

Management books are filled with stories of companies that have fired up their employees and reaped the rewards, or have ignored employees and failed. We have a host of our own stories, and we want to add yours to our list. Our winners list, that is.

Whether you're kicking off a departmental project, repairing a damaged financial situation, changing the culture, or even running a United Way campaign, you can gain support by using the suggestions in this book. We've seen it happen. We've made it happen. We know you can make it happen. All it takes is a spark.

Use two letters to turn "You're fired" into "You're fired up!" and you can trump Trump.

Internal marketing—it's a sure-fire bet. So, go on, get started. Strike your match, add some kindling, and watch the spark grow into a bonfire. And while you're at it, toast a few marshmallows. We'll be over shortly to help you celebrate.

Appendix

INTRODUCTION

The templates and tools included in the appendix section are some that we have developed and used throughout our projects. We hope they prove useful to you as you begin your own internal marketing initiatives.

Best Practices for Communicating Bad News

It's easy for us to communicate good news like a banner year, promotions, and business successes. However, communicating bad news during tough times can be very challenging. The right approach can help stabilize your workforce in these times and give employees some answers as well as relief from the anxiety they may feel.

The following are best practices to consider when communicating news through a period of change and transition.

1. Speak from the top down.
   - Employees will see that these communications are important.
   - Reassure employees that they are the most important asset you have to get through these times and encourage them to help the organization turn things around.
   - Arrange town hall meetings frequently during transition to get leaders in front of employees.

2. Supervisors and managers must be included early and there must be a plan to keep them fully informed throughout the transition.
   - They provide an opportunity for immediate, two-way communication with employees that others in the organization do not have on a frequent basis.
   - Employees need face-to-face communication as frequently as possible to enable them to provide feedback and ask questions.
3. When communicating, describe the news in a clear and straightforward manner.
   - Don't hide, minimize, or downplay the messages.
4. When communicating, make sure you explain why the changes are happening, who made the decisions, and what process was used.
   - Communication needs to answer, "How does this support the business goals?"
   - This demonstrates that leadership knows what they are doing and they have a solid plan.
5. Don't always rely on e-mail, especially to deliver bad news.
   - This vehicle increases the possibility that messages will be misinterpreted and the rumor mill will run amuck.

Communication Pictogram

These visuals are a good way for us and our clients to see just exactly what communications we are going to do for a given period. It givs us a gantt chart of sorts to be able to see all our events and make sure we're covering all the bases.

Appendix | 219

Stage 1 Communications Timeline – Sample

Activity	Nov 2003				Dec 2003				Jan 2004				Feb 2004				Mar 2004				Apr 2004		
Month/week beginning	3	10	17	24	1	8	15	22	29	5	12	19	26	2	9	16	23	1	8	15	22	29	5	12	19	26
XYZ *Initiative*																										
• Meeting	▲		▲		▲	▲	▲								◁		▲		▲	▲		▲	▲			
• Conf. call w/Execs	↻		↻		↻	↻	↻								↻		↻			↻						
XYZ Initiative Update							⊠												⊠							
Leadership memo + cascade																										
Communication/change assessment						▪														▪						
HR partner workshop			Focus groups																							
Communication tracking																										
Executive briefing and town halls (all staff)																										
• Exec call										↻																
• Organ. 1											▲															
• Organ. 2											▲															
• Organ. 3												▲														
• Organ. 4											⊠															
• Organ. 5													▲													
• International															▲											
Leadership/HR preparation																										
Executive briefing																						▲				
Organizational town hall mtgs. (led by BU exec)																								◁	◁	
BU leader comms																					▪▪▪					
Stage 2 workplan																										

▲ Scheduled meeting   ◁ Meeting, date TBD   ↻ Conference call   ⊠ E-mail   ▪ Holiday

COMMUNICATION STRATEGY

A communication strategy typically includes items like the goals of communication, your guiding principles, key messages, your audiences, and the communication events you will do. This is a high-level example showing what information you might want to include within each of those sections.

Goals of Communication Strategy

- Keep people informed on project status—across all organizations.
- Develop increasing commitment (from awareness to ownership) of project at all organizations by answering the question "what does this project mean to me?" for all audiences.
- Focus on communication to effectively prepare organizations for their rollouts.
- Focus on communication to build support for project for remaining organizations.
- Monitor effectiveness of communication.

Guiding Principles

- Clear messages using simple language
- Openness, honesty, credibility, and trust in all communications
- Two-way communication, with feedback valued and asked for
- Project Team and Management ownership of the communication program
- Ongoing commitment to the communications process

Effective Communication Guidelines

- There are multiple audiences for project communications.
- Communication needs to be:
  - Tailored to specific groups
  - Regular and informative
  - Real-time and relevant
- Communication content needs to be of interest to the target audience.
- Communication creates expectations.
- Regular communication should be delivered by the people who hold the most credibility with each stakeholder/audience group.
- Use change agents to get messages through informal channels.
- Communication needs to answer the question "What does it mean to me?"

Key Messages

- This plan will be the replicable process for future rollouts within the organizations.

Key Drivers for Change

- Business drivers:
  - Need to reduce costs
  - Need to meet customer requirements
  - Need to create common processes, systems, and shared data

Key Benefits

- Cost reductions

- Synergies among organizations
- Shared efficiencies in back office processes
- Improved information for analysis/decision making

Scope of Communication Activities

- Key project facts:
  - Timeline
  - Project Team
  - Activities to date
  - Current activities
- How this project will impact you:
  - Changes to what you do
  - Changes to how you do it
  - Opportunity to learn new skills
  - Increases cross-functional integration
  - Places organizations on one common system with secured, controlled access

Change Education

- Change is certain.
- Change is an opportunity to learn new skills.

How Employees Will Be Involved In Project

Type of Resource	Role Definition	Responsibilities
Management	• Project ownership & communication to drive change in the organization • Timely resolution of issues	• Support project with resources • Communication of project activities
Project Team	• Project ownership & communication to drive change in the organization • Analyze "current state" & develop "future state" business processes	• Day-to-day project tasks • Project design & ownership • Communication of project activities • Lead training of end users
Subject Matter Experts	• Provide detailed process or functional expertise, as needed • Awareness & support of project	• Join in meetings/conference calls with project team to provide input • Assist in simulation & testing
End Users	• Awareness & support of project	• Be trained on software • Learn new business processes

Key Communication Events

Event	Target Audience	Message Objective	Timing	Vehicles	Sender	Roles & Responsibilities
Project Intranet Web site	All audiences	• Build awareness • Explain vision, goals, scope, benefits, timeline • Present project team members • Explain vision, goals, scope, benefits, timeline, and status to date • Showcase project information concisely • Make presentations and deliverables public	Update as necessary, audit will take place every 2 weeks	Intranet	Communications team	The Web site houses all relevant project information in one collective area. Each subteam should have one delegate that is part of the communications team. This person is responsible for ensuring that deliverables from their team are reflected on the Web site. Communications team members will work with liaisons from each subteam to periodically (every 2 weeks) update the project Web site with deliverables.

Event	Target Audience	Message Objective	Timing	Vehicles	Sender	Roles & Responsibilities
News flash links	All audiences	• Build awareness around the project and share specific (highly related) information • Drive people to project Web site to get additional information • Educate, motivate, and excite users • Provide a high-level picture of accomplishments • Outline upcoming events/milestones • Explain vision, goals, scope, benefits, timeline, and status to date	Update as necessary	E-mail	Communications team	News flashes are a way to quickly highlight relevant project events in a quick summary format. This tool maintains users' awareness of project status and development and provides opportunity to voice concerns or issues that might be overlooked. This is also a method to draw users to the Web page. The Communications team can help draft messages initially, but eventually customer will assume this responsibility and the communications team will help coach and advise.

Event	Target Audience	Message Objective	Timing	Vehicles	Sender	Roles & Responsibilities
Frequently asked questions (FAQs)	All audiences	• Provides mechanism for users to pose questions to the project team about project • Answer questions as they arise • Also, questions and answers will be posted on the project Web site	Update as necessary	E-mail, project Web site	Communications team	Provides "real-time" answers to users' questions; helps increase awareness and understanding of project; results in increased participation of key users. All end users and team members should be encouraged to ask questions.
Issue tracker	Project team	• Project team members should be encouraged to log all significant issues and decisions into the Issue Tracker database as the preferred audit trail vehicle and as a way to communicate decisions to the rest of the team • This tool is a vehicle to communicate project decisions	Update as necessary (every day)	Access database	Project management	Project management should encourage the widespread use of this tool and timely resolution of issues.

Event	Target Audience	Message Objective	Timing	Vehicles	Sender	Roles & Responsibilities
Monthly project update newsletter	Company executives and officers, BPOs, end users	• Provide general awareness regarding project objectives, timelines, upcoming activities • Share success stories/quick wins • Drive people to go to project Web site for additional information • The status reports maintain awareness of project status and success and help to keep the project visible	Once per month (distributed 3rd week of each month)	E-mail	Project communications team: may be sent through executive sponsor	The communications team can help draft messages initially, but eventually customer will assume this responsibility and the communications team will help coach and advise.
Monthly project update presentation (What it means to me)	BPOs, end users	• Provide information on topics describing how individuals will be affected	Once per month (distributed 4th week of each month)	Sent in hard copy or e-mail format	Project communications team: may be sent through executive sponsor	The communications team can help draft presentations initially, but eventually customer will assume this responsibility and the communications team will help coach and advise.

Event	Target Audience	Message Objective	Timing	Vehicles	Sender	Roles & Responsibilities
Team lead meetings	All project team leads	• Allow project management to address issues relating to moving forward with the project • Keep project management informed of developments on the communications team and other subteams	Brief meeting on weekly basis	Meetings/conference calls	Leads of each functional and technical team	Project management should structure an agenda for each meeting. Communications team member should take minutes of each meeting and distribute it to all team members. Each team lead should be encouraged to relay news back to members of their subteam.
One-on-one coaching	Functional and technical project team leads	• Periodically talk to functional and technical leads to address any project issues that may come up • Answer any questions that they may have • Ensure leads and team members understand and buy-in to rationale for program decisions • Find out about any pressing concerns that the leads have uncovered	As needed (every other week)	One-on-one meetings	Functional and technical project team leads and other project team members	Experienced leads should be mentors to others on team. Their role is to check in with them periodically to see how things are progressing and if any pressing issues have come up. It is also a way for us to gauge how affected end users are responding to communication efforts and a way for us to gauge project perception.

Event	Target Audience	Message Objective	Timing	Vehicles	Sender	Roles & Responsibilities
Team-building activities	Entire project team	• Facilitate team building • Develop unity throughout the project • Allow all project members to meet and get to know one another	Once a month or as needed–close to project milestones	Various activities (both on- and off-site)	Project management/communications team	Project management should try to maintain high energy levels and morale among project team members through team development activities. In addition, team-building promotes the working relationships of individual teams and promotes group cohesiveness–which is essential for long-term projects.
Project team calendar	Entire project team	• Keeps entire team informed of who is going to be on-site any given day • Facilitates meeting schedules, work activity, and communication	Update as necessary (daily)	Team calendar	Entire project team and administered by admin	The calendar helps all team members be aware of one another's individual schedules. It also notes key project events. Project management should encourage all project team members to update the calendar frequently.

Event	Target Audience	Message Objective	Timing	Vehicles	Sender	Roles & Responsibilities
Project management team weekly conference call	Executives and project management	• Discuss issues and exchange updates on project status • Decide on topics and issues for main Tuesday conference call	Mondays 1:00 – 2:00	Conference call	PMO or executive sponsor	This is a mechanism to discuss any issues and updates in preparation for the main conference call occurring on Tuesday mornings each week. PMO should initiate and lead weekly calls.
Main weekly project update conference call	Executive sponsor, steering committee, all BPOs, project management, and project leads	• Update BPOs, steering committee, executive sponsor once a week via a conference call to keep them abreast of project issues, progress, and status • The calls should focus on providing progress reports, sharing key decisions, and helping them understand critical issues. The purpose of the calls is to keep these individuals engaged and ensure they are getting appropriate (i.e., direct) information about the project • Answer any questions that they may have	Tuesdays 11:00 AM – 12:00 PM	Conference calls	PMO or executive sponsor	This is a mechanism to develop key awareness and understanding of the project. It also provides the leaders with an opportunity to voice concerns or issues that may have been overlooked to the attention of project management. PMO should initiate and lead weekly calls. PMO will follow up with the team regarding any concerns that have come up based on the conference calls.

Event	Target Audience	Message Objective	Timing	Vehicles	Sender	Roles & Responsibilities
Technical team weekly conference call	PMO and technical team leads/member	• Discuss technical issues • Update weekly progress	Thursdays 9:00 AM – 10:30 AM	Conference call	PMO	This is a mechanism to discuss technical infrastructure issues and receive updates on weekly progress. PMO should initiate and lead weekly calls.

SPEECH EXAMPLE

A lot of times, as communication experts, we're called on to write a president's talking points and speeches for meetings, conference calls, and other communication events. We did not write this particular one; however, we think this is a good example of a speech that inspired and informed, and we wanted to share it with you.

Sample Inspirational Speech

> Remarks
> President Richard A. Berman
> Homecoming 2004

Good morning. On behalf of the board of trustees, the faculty, the staff, and most of all the students, welcome parents, and welcome alumni. Welcome to *your* college . . . for Homecoming 2004.

It is so gratifying to see so many of you here.

In four months, I will begin my tenth year as president of a college that had a very impressive past—and had the potential to be exactly the kind of college the world needs in the 21st century.

Nine years ago, I made many promises and many commitments. I made myself accountable to the alumni, to Manhattanville's trustees and faculty, and staff and students. I made myself accountable to YOU.

I outlined my vision for Manhattanville.

It is a vision rooted in the concept of the liberal arts college as an agent of change; as a repository of academic excellence that seeks and achieves the full and active engagement with the world.

It is a vision that acknowledges the ultimate supremacy of the human spirit.

It's a vision that asserts that we cannot be an institution in isolation. But rather, we must be a catalyst for change in our community.

This vision—which is now OUR VISION TOGETHER—ensures that our students receive a spectacular academic education in an environment where they can learn about *themselves* . . . where they can work and play and live effectively in a *diverse* community . . . where they have *learned* a sense of purpose and *leave* with an understanding of their responsibility to make the world a better place.

NINE years ago—I think I even said it FIVE years ago—one of Manhattanville's biggest problems was that we were a well-kept secret.

Well, as many of you know, that is no longer the case!

- *U.S. News & World Report* ranks us in the "top tier" of our peer institutions.
- Kaplan, one of the leading guidebook companies, considers us one of the "320 Most Interesting Colleges."
- *Princeton Review* says we're one of the "Best 351 Colleges in the Nation." And it ranked our professors number 18 in the country—along with Middlebury and Smith and Wellesley—for "Bringing Learning to Life."
- And *The Fiske Guide* named us one of just 22 private colleges in the nation that is a "BEST BUY." Now that's got to make parents feel good!

So I guess our secret is out!

Over the past nine years, we've made so much progress as an institution.

- We've revitalized our core values, resulting in our clear and concise mission statement: *to educate ethically and socially responsible leaders for the global community.*

- We've retained our best faculty, and strengthened our numbers—adding 36 new full-time members and bringing our total to 84.
- We've improved our facilities, little by little. We renovated our photography studio, dance studio, and ceramics lab. We built a music recording studio and a working television studio.
- We've added our gorgeous new Library Café, and expanded our hours to 24 hours a day.
- We've dramatically improved our technology across the campus, resulting in *Yahoo!* magazine naming us one of the "100 Most Wired" colleges in the country.
- We've endowed two chairs—in economics and in Christian philosophy—to help us sustain those important areas of study.
- We've raised millions of dollars for scholarships, so we can make Manhattanville affordable for deserving young people.
- And we received our first one-time, million-dollar donation, from Nancy Roberts King, which she dedicated to our library.
- We have more than *tripled* our endowment.
- We have more than *tripled* our net assets.
- And, we have operated *in the black* for each of the past eight years.

So where does that put us today?

- The Class of 2007—our fall freshmen—are some of the brightest and most socially aware students we have ever had. Half of them ranked in our top two tiers academically, which is more than ever before. Many held significant leadership and service positions in high school. One student is the New York State Youth of the Year, based on her exemplary character and superior leadership skills. Among our board of trustees scholars, we also welcome a solo violinist who plays with the Puerto Rico Symphonic Orchestra; a musical theatre director and performer from San Francisco who trained at Carnegie Mellon; and an All-State soccer player from Kentucky who has been president of several student organizations while also serving Oxfam, Special Olympics, Habitat for Humanity, and several other organizations. We welcome four more Seeds of Peace students from the Middle East, as well as students from around the world, including Italy, Haiti, Spain, and Bangladesh.

- *Many people want to come here.* We received almost 3,000 applications for 420 spots, which was more than ever before.
- In all, Manhattanville has 1,500 full-time undergraduate students, from 37 states and 53 nations. Our students continue to pursue their passions while they are here—in clubs and on athletics teams, on stage, or on our campus radio station.
- We also have 1,000 part-time graduate students on our campus.
- We offer more than 50 undergraduate areas of study, including literature, the classics, and romance languages—as you remember. We've added music management, communication, graphic design, and many others as well. And if this isn't enough, students can "self-design" their own majors.
- Our students also learn through internships at more than 350 institutions, including the Metropolitan Museum of Art, Major League Baseball, MasterCard, and Merrill Lynch.
- They study "abroad" in Japan and South Africa and elsewhere in the world. They live and study in New York City, in our Semester in the City program.
- They participate in "service-learning" through the many programs here and abroad that are sponsored by our Duchesne Center for Religion and Social Justice.
- Recent graduates have gone on to *great graduate schools,* including Yale, Georgetown, Cornell Law School, Carnegie Mellon, Johns Hopkins, Stanford, NYU, and Juilliard.

- And even in this very tough market, many of our May 2003 graduates are working—in teaching, insurance, accounting, music management, sales and marketing, financial services, and travel. Many are engaged in direct community service.

We are extremely proud of our students and our alumni.

And Manhattanville is on a solid, stable ground—academically and financially.

So where do we go from here? As I see it, we have two choices. We can be content with the improvements we have made, or we can challenge ourselves to take this college to the next level—to reach for greatness.

To be great means attracting and retaining the best students and faculty possible.

To be great means making Manhattanville the best it can be in every way—academically, artistically, socially, athletically, financially, *and ethically and morally*.

Greatness requires having a *library* that rivals the best college libraries in the nation.

Greatness requires a *state-of-the-art science building*.

Greatness requires a new performing arts center.

Greatness requires giving the students *a place they can call their own*, where they can socialize and dream and plan their futures.

Greatness requires giving our student athletes better equipment and new facilities.

Greatness requires having an endowment that will let us enrich our academics and continue to grow and innovate.

And finally, *greatness* will require that everyone in this room—everyone in the entire Manhattanville community—participate in the journey.

We are very appreciative of our core of dedicated donors.

But it must grow! I believe it will grow, and I hope it will include each and every one of you.

Now is the time to focus your energy and your spirit of generosity right here at Manhattanville College.

Today, I am asking you to demonstrate to each other, and to our students, that you recognize opportunity when you see it.

You have faith that greatness is possible, and that greatness is possible *here.*

We have never had a more important job.

We have never had a greater opportunity to preserve the legacy of Manhattanville.

Every one of us is a steward of this great institution—its students, its campus, its history, and most of all, its future.

Please demonstrate your commitment to our mission.

Please participate in restoring the ties between the past, the present, and the future.

I am asking for your help, your support, your guidance, and your prayers. I ask you to stand up and be counted—as friends, as colleagues, and as partners.

Think of any "great" college. It didn't get that way without the active and generous support of its alumni and its parents.

With your support, together we will succeed in this great collaborative adventure.

Because:

- *Together,* we dream.
- *Together,* we embrace greatness.
- And *together,* we believe in Manhattanville College.

Thank you.

STAKEHOLDER ANALYSIS

We use this stakeholder analysis template at the very beginning of our planning to ensure we understand who our audiences are and what we need to do to gain their respective level of commitment for the given initiative. Many times your audiences will need to have varying degrees of commitment. The ones who are required to take action or will be affected most will need to be more committed than groups who need to just be informed of what is going on. This tool helps you to determine who needs to be at what level and then, subsequently, provide a plan for how you will achieve that.

Appendix | 239

1. Objective of the document:

The entire document will lay a foundation for the **communication strategy and plan**.
The "Level of Impact" column can feed into the existing **training strategy and plan**.

Common Stakeholders for initiatives

Stakeholders	# Emp.	Level of Impact Low (L) Medium (M) High (H)	Current Stakeholder Profile	Current Level of Commitment Awareness (A) Understanding (U) Buy-in (B) Commitment (C)	Desired Level of Commitment Awareness (A) Understanding (U) Buy-in (B) Commitment (C)	Preliminary Action Steps (How do we move them from Current to Desired Commitment level?)
Executives	4	H	Has heard of initiative through meetings but does not understand it	A	A, U, B, C	1. Hold meetings with executives one-on-one to gain their support. 2. Have them do communications cascade to their respective organizations.
Directors	15	H	May not be aware of initiative	None	A, U, B, C	3. Hold meetings with all directors to explain their role in the initiative. 4. Create communications cascade process for them in order to share with staff.
Staff	2000	L	No awareness of initiative	None	A, U	5. Hold informational session explaining the initiative.

SURVEY EXAMPLE

Surveying is so critical to understanding if your internal marketing plan is on track and achieving your goals. This is a sample survey to show you some of the questions we might use to determine how employees are receiving the communications as well as the overall internal marketing initiative. Surveys are a good way to show employees that you are interested in their perspective and feedback.

Sample e-Survey

Quantitative Feedback

Each of the following statements will have five multiple-choice measurements:

- Strongly agree
- Agree
- Partly agree/partly disagree
- Disagree
- Strongly disagree

1. I believe that [xyz] is an important initiative for us at this time.
2. I'm excited about being a part of [xyz initiative].
3. I understand what I need to do to support [xyz initiative].
4. I feel like I received the right amount and kind of communication to implement [xyz initiative].
5. My team members and I can make emotional connections with our customers on a regular basis.

Qualitative Feedback (open-ended questions)

Each of the following questions will feature an open text box in which the respondent can enter free-text answers.

6. What are some of the ways you and your team connect with customers?
7. What would make it easier for you to connect with customers?
8. What can we [leadership, corporate, department, etc.] do, in terms of the way we communicate about [xyz initiative], to help you be as effective as possible?
9. Do you have any other questions we can help answer?

Sample E-mail Text Inviting to Survey

Dear [Audience],

I want to thank all of you for your participation in [meeting, call, etc.]. I hope you enjoyed celebrating our successes so far, sharing tips and feedback with us and other employees, and learning about our new changes to the company. We're very excited about what we've already achieved with [initiative]—thanks to all your hard work—and what's coming up next! Thank you for playing such an important role in this exciting venture!

We will all be getting together again in a couple of months to talk more about other new changes. In the meantime, I'd like your participation in one more thing that will help us make [initiative] and [company] be the best that it can be.

Please take five minutes by [date] to complete a short e-survey regarding our [meeting, call, etc.] and initiative.

The survey can be found at [survey link].

Thank you once again for your active participation in what will be, without a doubt, an unprecedented milestone in [company's] history. I look forward to working with each of you to [Slogan].

Warm Regards,

Mr. or Ms. Executive

TRAINING SELECTION MATRIX

This has proved a helpful tool when trying to determine the best way to deliver training solutions. Remember, the instructor-led method isn't effective for every type of training just as e-learning is not. Use this tool to help you weigh the pros and cons of each.

Training Solutions Selection Matrix

Training Delivery Options

Delivery Method	Primary Strength	Primary Weakness	Relative Cost to Develop/Deploy	Ability to Scale	Ease of Update	Mode	Modularity	Informational	Procedural	Behavioral	Conceptual
Instructor-led (ILT)	Familiarity and interaction	Ability to scale; total cost of delivery	Low/Medium	*	***	Sync	*	*	*	**	**
Text-based (job aid, comm plan)	Portable, universally available	Timeliness, no interaction or feedback	Low/Low	**	**	Async	***	***	**	**	***
Broadband network w/live or prerecorded video	Strengths of ILT, plus scalable, high-quality video capability	Technology not universally deployed	Low/High	**	**	Both	* (Sync) ** (Async)	**	**	***	**
Virtual classrooms w/voice over IP, Web slide shows, conferences	Strength of broadband, plus common technology	Some technologies are dependent on Internet traffic, some shift in classroom metaphor	Low/Low	***	***	Both	* (Sync) ** (Async)	***	***	**	*
On-the-Job Training (OJT)	Provides just-in-time coaching, training, and feedback	Dependent upon SME serving as coach	Low/Low	***	***	Sync	***	*	**	***	*
Electronic performance support (EPS)	Driven by the user; provides just-in-time "bites" of information	Stays within an application	Medium/Low	**	**	Async	***	***	***	*	***
CD-ROM/ CBT/WBT	Engaging, can be highly interactive to a range of learners, disconnected	Time to develop, hard to update	High/Low	**	*	Async	***	***	***	**	***

Scale: Less efficient = *   Most efficient = ***

Appendix   243

Terms

Informational	Sharing facts
Procedural	Linking action steps together to form a process; requires practice to learn; job aids to reinforce
Behavioral	Similar to procedural but requires more options; role playing and simulation are used to learn, reinforce by practice
Conceptual	Permits learner to extrapolate from the known to the unknown. Required to practice and a high degree of interaction.
Asynchronous	Recorded session to allow users to attend or view content at any time
Synchronous	Live session with instructor

Bibliography

Baldoni, John. "Effective Leadership Communications: It's More Than Talk." *Harvard Management Communication Letter* 5, No. 4, April 2002: 2.

Boone, Louis E. *Quotable Business.* Random House, 1992, 151.

Cochrane, Amanda. "Management Maketh Man—How the Hell Does Branson Manage it?" Director Annual Convention Special (Institute of Directors, April 1994). *Management Weekly,* July 1991.

Coffman, Curt and Gabriel Gonzalez-Molina. *Follow This Path: How the World's Greatest Organizations Drive Growth by Unleashing Human Potential.* Warner Business Books, 2002, 142.

Dolliver, Mark. "Call it Anti-Brand Loyalty." *AdWeek,* June 11, 2001. http://www.vnuemedia.com

Hollis, Emily. "Southwest Airlines: Employee Education Takes Flight." *Chief Learning Officer Magazine,* September 2003. http://www.clomedia.com

Kelleher, Herb. "A Culture of Commitment by Herb Kelleher," *Leader to Leader.* No. 4, Spring 1997: 20–24.

Kirkpatrick, Donald L. *Evaluating Training Programs: The Four Levels.* 2nd ed. Berrett-Koehler, 1998.

Mercer Human Resource Consulting Press Release. "Employees Value Effective Communication from Their Employer." April 17, 2003. http://www.mercerhr.com

Neff, Thomas J., and James M. Citrin. *Lessons from the Top, Currency.* Doubleday/Random House, 1999, 190.

Question.com Web site. http://www.question.com/quotes/authors/dwight_d_eisenhower.html

Service Management Group Web site. "Bill Fromm." http://www.servicemanagement.com

Singapore Airlines Web site. Careers. http://www.singaporeair.com

Stewart. "A New 500 for the New Economy." *Fortune,* May 15, 1995.

Yi, Matthew. "Intel Boss Puts it Bluntly in Letter to Employees, Barrett Says Firm's Missteps are Unacceptable." *San Francisco Chronicle,* July 28, 2004. http://www.sfgate.com/cgi-bin/article.cgi?file=/chronicle/archive/2004/07/28/BUGTO7U3HQ1.DTL

Index

A
Accountability, 23–24
Adams, Scott, 36, 142
Adversity, 10–11
Advertising, word-of-mouth, 29
Adweek, 26
AmeriCares, 35
Apple Computers, 18, 51–52
Apprentice, The, 214–15
Audience, 82–91
    contract workers, 91
    direct effect, 87
    needs of, 83
    nonemployee workers, 89–90
    off-site workers, 88–89
    positioning and, 85–86
    second and third shifts, 88
    varying message by audience, 84–85
Auditory media, 104
Austin, Nancy, 79
Awareness, 54–56

B
Barkley Evergreen & Partners Inc., 4, 25
Barrett, Craig, 11
Bass, 18
Berman, Richard, 61, 232
Block, Peter, 175
Boston Beer Company, 169, 193–95
Boys & Girls Clubs of America, 42
Brand/branding
    see also Internal brand
    auditory media and, 104
    early efforts in, 174–76
    "E" employees and, 44–45
    e-mail and, 119
    employee love for, 3
    marketing. *See* Marketing
    promise(s), 4–5, 6, 26
    visual media and, 103–4
Branson, Richard, 45, 56
Bulletin boards, 122
Burson-Marsteller, 172
Business performance, 33–34
Business TV, 114–15
BusinessWeek TV, 36–37

C
Career development/planning, 150, 151
Catherine the Great, 22
Celebrity spokespersons, 130–31
Champions, 127–31
    finding, 128–29
    spokespersons/mascots, 130–31
    support from, 129–31
Change
    communication and, 207
    culture and, 11, 54
    employee anxiety and, 161–62
City Slickers, 145–46
Climate assessment, 91–93
Coaching, 153–54
Coca-Cola, 64, 104
Coffman, Curt, 37
Communication, 95–126
    bulletin boards, 122
    business TV, 114–15
    in company meetings, 112–13
    of company news, 109–10
    conference calls, 115–16
    dealing with good/bad news, 99–101, 217–18
    defining key messages, 96–99
    of detailed factual information, 111

Communication, *continued*
  e-mail, 118-19
  employee recognition, 108-9
  etiquette, 105
  of financial information, 111
  internal brand and, 53
  intranet, 119-20
  knowledge of audience and, 82-86
  of management directives, 112
  match vehicles to message, 102-4, 126
  of mission/vision/values, 105-7
  of motivational information, 107-8
  newsletters, 117-18
  one on one, 121
  overcommunication, 144-45
  perspective, 96-98
  pictogram, 218-19
  plan execution and, 132-33
  PowerPoint, 123-25
  print piece/letter, 116-17
  of strategic information, 108
  strategy, 220-31
  targeted, 208
  of training information, 111
  unusual means of sharing, 122
  videoconference/web conference, 113-14
Community, sense of, 19
Community of practice, 167
Community relations, 199-201
Company meetings, 112-13
Company news, 109-10
Company philosophy, 158-60
Compensation, 35, 36-37
Cone, Fairfax, 102
Conference calls, 115-16
Confucius, 166
Consistency, 54-56
Contract workers, 91
Cordell, Phil, 15, 58
Cortell, Gary, 36, 40
Cost
  of low productivity, 39
  of turnover, 37-38
Cross-training, 151. *See also* Training

Culture, 11-14, 54
Customer loyalty, 52
Customer satisfaction, 34
  "E" employees and, 44-48
  feeling of welcome, 47-48

D

Daly, Jerry, 172-74
Dechert LLP, 63
Denison, Daniel, 71
Department to department (D2D), 171-80
  benefits of, 177
  branding and, 174-76
Dilbert cartoon strip, 142
Doubletree Hotels, 104
"Driving Literacy Home," 200
Duncan, Bill, 8-9

E

Eastern Airlines, 25
"E" employees, 34-35
  see also Employee(s)
  customer satisfaction and, 44-48
  effect of, on group, 41-42
  high performance of, 39-40
"E" environment
  behaviors, 3, 16
  creating, 16-24
  employees and, 14-16
  factors. *See* Factors, "E" environment
Employee(s)
  see also "E" employees
  attracting/retaining talent, 54, 59
  brand loyalty and, 52
  brand promise and, 4-5, 26
  considered biggest assets of company, 5-11
  feelings communicated by, 55-56
  recognition of. *See* Rewards/recognition
  retention rates, 34
  satisfaction, 34
  training. *See* Training
  turnover, 40

80/20 principle, 26-27
Einstein, Albert, 22
Eisenhower, Dwight D., 148
Electronic surveys, 136, 240-41
Elizabeth Arden, 14-15
E-mail communication, 118-19
Employee-of-the-month program, 188-89
Empower, 22-23, 35, 46
    flexibility and, 22-23
    risk taking, 23
Enable, 19-22, 35, 45-46
    making vision a reality, 20-21
    with training/work environment, 21-22
Engage, 17-19, 45
Ensure, 23-24
Entertainment companies, 192
Environment, work, 21
Evaluation
    of behavior, 164-65
    of learning, 164
    results and impact, 165-66
    training reaction, 163
Experiential learning, 166
Extended stay hotels, 6-10

F
Factors, "E" environment, 16-24
    empower, 22-23
    enable, 19-22
    engage, 17-19
    ensure, 23-24
Factual information, 111
Fashion companies, 192
FedEx, 6, 31-33, 44-45, 48-49, 57, 63, 199-200
Feedback, 137, 153, 163
Fields, Debbi, 104
Financial information, 111
Fiorina, Carly, 12
Flagstone Hospitality Management, 186-88
"Flawless consulting," 175
Flexibility, 22
Focus groups, 136-37
Foreshadowing, 134

Fortune magazine 100 Best Companies list, 33, 59
Fox, Michael J., 130
Frequent flier points, 191-92
Fromm, Bill, 25
Future Business Leaders of America, 43

G
Gallup Poll, 37, 39
Gap Inc., 148-49, 157-58
Goals, 79-80
    employee contribution to, 25-27
    employee recognition and, 188-89
Goldman, Seth, 196-97
Gonzalez-Molina, Gabriel, 37
Growth, professional, 38-39
Gunning-Fog Index, 142-43

H
Hampton Inn, 15, 22-23, 28-29, 58-59, 63, 90
Hard-copy surveys, 136
Herrmann, Alex, 120
Hewlett-Packard, 11-12
Hill, Mike, 38, 106, 153-54
Hilton Hotels Corporation, 6-10, 90, 96
Holiday Inn hotels, 17-18, 172-74, 174-76, 199, 215
Holthouser, Jim, 6-10
Homewood Suites by Hilton, 6-10, 11, 200
Honest Tea, 196-97
Huang, Phyllis, 148-49, 157
Hutcheson, Dan, 11

I
IBM, 38, 153-54
    communication of company values, 105-7
    On Demand Workplace intranet, 119-20
Inc. magazine's Regional Entrepreneur of the Year, 25
Intel, 10-11, 104

Internal brand
  see also Brand/branding
  advantages of, 52–59
  appearance of, 62–63
  awareness/consistency and, 54–56
  Coca-Cola, 64
  creating, 59–64
  driving change with, 57–59
  and external brand compared, 60
  McDonald's, 65
  Microsoft, 65
  Nike, 65
  quiz, 66–69
  Sony, 64–65
  sustaining positive culture with, 56–57
Internal marketing
  business performance and, 33–34
  choosing your champions, 127–31
  climate assessment, 91–93
  D2D. *See* Department to department (D2D)
  defined, 3–5
  executing the plan, 132–35
  goals and objectives, 79–81
  implementation steps, 71–72
  management/culture and, 12–14
  measuring/adapting the plan, 135–37
  need for, 27–29
  setting course from A to B, 72–81
  targeting, 87–91
  types of, 6
International Institute for Management Development, 71
Internship, 152
Interviews, 137
Intranet communication, 119–20

J

Jacobs, Bill, 41
Job rotation, 151
Jobs, Steve, 18, 51
Johnson & Johnson, 173
Jovovich, Milla, 130

K

Kelleher, Herb, 57, 152, 168
Kessler, Barrie, 40
Ketchum PR firm, 32
King, Jeff, 4–5
Kirkpatrick, Donald, 163
Koch, Jim, 193–94

L

Leisure companies, 191–92
Lesher, Lynn, 208–9
Letters, 116–17
Levi Strauss and Company, 156–57
Lobo, Glyn, 63
Lockhart, Gene, 41
Logos, 62

M

Management directives, 112
Manhattanville College, 61–62, 232–37
March of Dimes, 199
Marketing, 140–46
  alignment, 140–41
  communication, 144–45
  to internal audiences, 82–86
  persistence and consistency, 141–42
  simple sells, 142–44
Marriott, Bill, 45
Mascots, 130–31
Maslow, Abraham, 83
Maslow's hierarchy of needs, 83, 96
MasterCard International, 41
McDonald's, 65
Measurement (of results)
  measurement plan logistics, 138
  planning tools for, 137
  schedule, 139
  techniques, 136–37
Memory, human, 104
Memphis in May event, 195
Mentoring, 154
Mercer Consulting, 34–35
Microsoft, 65

Microsoft PowerPoint, 114, 123-25
Milt, Amber, 36-37, 40
Mission, 105-7
Mock, Angie, 176, 186-88
Motivation, 39
    communication and, 107-8
    inspirational speech example, 232-37
M.S. Carriers, 207-10
Music, 104
Music companies, 192

N

NBC, 104
Negativity, 21
Newsletters, 117-18
Night shift workers, 88
Nike, 65
Nonprofit companies, 192-93

O

Objectives, 79-81
Obstacles, overcoming, 197-99
Office politics, 21
Olfactory messages, 104
O'Neil, Buck, 130
On-the-spot awards, 193
Opinions, 129
Opportunities, analyzing, 75-76
Optimism, 21-22
Orientation, 155-58
Orwell, George, 193
Out of the box thinking, 22

P

Palmisano, Sam, 106, 120
Passion for Excellence, A (Peters and Austin), 79
Perkins Restaurants, 210-11
Peters, Tom, 79
Petree, Fritz, 159
Philosophy, of company, 158-60
Phone conference, 108
Positioning, 85-86
PowerPoint, 114, 123-25
Pride, 39
Print pieces, 116-17
Professional services companies, 192
Promus Hotels, 96
Public displays of affection, 190-91

Q-R

Quality programs, 212-14
Quiz, internal brand, 66-69
Reading levels, 142-44
Real Heroes of Business and Not a CEO Among Them (Fromm), 25
Reputation, 48
Retail companies, 192
Rewards/recognition, 133, 181-201
    choices, 190-201
    communication of, 108-9
    company culture and, 186-88
    company goals and, 188-90
    framework of, 183-87
    rules of, 182-83
    sincerity and timeliness of, 182
Risk taking, 23
Ritz-Carlton, 47

S

Salaries, 35, 36-37
Samuel Adams beer, 193
Sarjoo, Vic, 42, 43-44
Seinfeld, Jerry, 130
Self-esteem, 38
Sense of entitlement mentality, 197
Setting course, 72-81
    analysis of situation, 72-73
    SWOT analysis, 73-78
Sharing ownership, 196-97
SIA Group, 149
Singapore Airlines, 149
Skills training, 158-60. *See also* Training
SMART objectives, 80-81
Social network, 167-68
Sony, 64-65
SoundExchange, 40, 192
Southwest Airlines, 25, 48-49, 56-57, 59, 152, 159-60, 168
Speech, inspirational, 232-37
Spokespersons, 130-31
Sprint, 18-19
Stakeholder analysis, 238-39
Starnes, Michael, 207

Stovall, Calvin, 8–9
Strategic information, communicating, 108
Street, Picabo, 130
Strengths, analyzing, 73
Success, measuring, 23
Succession planning, 150
Sugars, Adrian, 6, 10
Surveys, 136, 240–41
SWOT analysis, 73–80
    opportunities, 75–76
    strengths, 73
    threats, 76–78
    weaknesses, 74–75

T

Television, business, 114–15
Ten Commandments of Business and How to Break Them, The (Fromm), 25
Threats, analyzing, 76–78
Training, 147–69
    coaching, 153–54
    communication and, 111
    cross-training, 151
    dual marketing benefit of, 148
    employees as company reps, 160
    employees as trainers, 168
    employee security and, 161–62
    enabling with, 21–22
    evaluating. *See* Evaluation
    experiential learning, 166
    fun in, 169
    internal brand and, 53
    marketing internally/externally, 166–67
    as marketing tool, 148
    mentoring, 154
    at orientation, 155–58
    skills training and company philosophy, 158–60
    social network and, 167–68
    training selection matrix, 242–44
Travel companies, 191–92
True life situations, 203–15
    midsize merger, 204–7
    M.S. Carriers, 207–10
    Perkins Restaurants, 210–11
    quality program initiatives, 212–14
Trump, Donald, 214–15
Turnover, cost of, 37–38

U–V

U.S. News & World Report, 61
Values, 105–7
Videoconferences, 113–14
Virgin, 45, 48–49, 56
Vision
    communicating, 105–7
    employee rewards/recognition and, 189
Visual media, 103–4
VLSI Research, 11
VSAM Global Asset Management, 43–44

W–Z

WalkAmerica campaign, 199–200
Weaknesses, analyzing, 74–75
Webcast, 107
Web conferences, 113–14
Welling, Curtis R., 35
Williams, Venus, 130
Wilson, Kemmons, 17–18
Wilson, Michael, 28
Word-of-mouth advertising, 29
World Championship Barbecue Cooking Contest, 195–96
Wozniak, Steve, 51
Zeta-Jones, Catherine, 130

Breinigsville, PA USA
11 April 2011
259624BV00006B/3/P